# SEVEN HOLY WOMEN

*Conversations with Saints and Friends*

*Melinda Johnson*

*Georgia Briggs*
*Katherine Bolger Hyde*
*Laura S. Jansson*
*Summer Kinard*
*Melissa Elizabeth Naasko*
*Anna Neill*

ANCIENT F/  N, INDIANA

Seven Holy Women: Conversations with Saints and Friends
Copyright ©2020 Ancient Faith Publishing

All rights reserved. No part of this publication may be reproduced by any means, electronic, mechanical, photocopying, recording, scanning, or otherwise, without the prior written permission of the Publisher.

Published by:
　Ancient Faith Publishing
　A Division of Ancient Faith Ministries
　P.O. Box 748
　Chesterton, IN 46304

ISBN: 978-1-944967-85-7

Library of Congress Control Number: 2020944834

Printed in the United States of America

*Now, therefore, you are no longer strangers and foreigners, but fellow citizens with the saints and members of the household of God, having been built on the foundation of the apostles and prophets, Jesus Christ Himself being the chief cornerstone, in whom the whole building, being fitted together, grows into a holy temple in the Lord, in whom you also are being built together for a dwelling place of God in the Spirit.*

*(Ephesians 2:19–22)*

For Carina, with thanks for what she has taught me about unselfish love.
—Melinda

For Brigid, who will tell it to you straight. —Georgia

For my daughters, Lena and Elizabeth. We have all struggled with the dragon, but in Christ we shall prevail! —Katherine

For Mother Helena, in thanksgiving for the love and prayers you offer for me, my family, and the world. —Laura

For Nana Helen, who invited me into her friendship with the saints. —Summer

For my husband, who reminds me to be a better person than I would ordinarily be. —Melissa

For the young ladies at St. Raphael: thank you for the journey toward knowing the saints. —Anna

For Beth and Jen, whose faith and friendship have supported and inspired me for twenty-seven years. —Molly

## Contents

Prologue   9
How to Read and Write This Book   11

STONE   ~   *Laura S. Jansson*   13
You Are Morwenna   15
On the Life of the Saint   20
Water and Stone   25
My Stones, My Cliff, My Church   32
Building a Wall Together   34
Between the Rock and the Hard Place   36

SONG   ✣   *Georgia Briggs*   39
You Are Kassiani   41
On the Life of the Saint   47
The Better Things   51
Turning Down the Apple   56
Beautiful Struggle   58
The Song of Your Life   60

LEAF   ♦   *Molly Sabourin*   63
You Are Ia   65
On the Life of the Saint   70
A Miraculous Voyage   72
A Resurrection of Hope   79
A Leap of Faith   81
A Gift of Stillness   83

DREAM   ☽   *Anna Neill*   87
You Are Nino   89

On the Life of the Saint   94
Daring to Dream with Saint Nino   99
Dream the Hard Things   104
Awakening Lost Dreams   106
Your Mission, Should You Choose to Accept It   108

RIVER ⌒ *Summer Kinard*   111
You Are Piama   113
On the Life of the Saint   122
Settling Down with God   126
Expecting God   132
Building Her Faith   134
God Is with You   136

DRAGON ♦ *Katherine Bolger Hyde*   139
You Are Margaret   141
On the Life of the Saint   146
Battling the Ugly Beast   150
Here There Be Dragons   154
Lending a Trusty Sword   156
Recognizing Dragons   158

FLOWER ❦ *Melissa Elizabeth Naasko*   161
You Are Casilda de Toledo   163
On the Life of the Saint   167
A Dinner Party   170
Befores and Afters   173
Speaking to Our Sisters   175
Seeking Hidden Treasure   177

HOME ⚱ *Melinda Johnson*   181
You Are You   183
The Women Who Wrote This Book   187

# *Prologue*

PERHAPS YOU ARE one of us—the quiet majority—who longs for a more profound experience of faith but resists, for her own good reasons, the effort of seeking one. Perhaps you are worried this book will land on the tottering pile on your nightstand, where you keep the stories you wish you could tell yourself. Perhaps you are seeking encouragement from strong, joyful companions who remind you of the holy treasure in your tired heart.

This book is for you. Yes, even you—the cautious, curious, weary, skeptical woman who can't decide if she's going to read the rest of this small paragraph. You.

Between the title page and the final page, you will open an immersive, imaginative journey into your spiritual life. You will read the stories of other women as your own story. You will be Morwenna, Kassiani, Ia, Nino, Piama, Margaret, and Casilda. You will find the stones you are carrying to build a church. You will hear the song you are writing and the emperor you are escaping. You will breathe the prayer that will topple idols. You will confront a prison cell and a dragon. You will hold your enemies frozen in their tracks and see danger transformed to fragrant roses in your hands.

You will read and write your own story. And, like us, you will find these seven beautiful women lingering with you after the stories are told and the book is closed.

# *How to Read and Write This Book*

READ ALONE OR with a group of friends—a book club, a parish group, or your girls'-night-out posse. Start at the beginning, with Morwenna. Read her chapter together or alone and write your own answers to the Personal Survey questions. Pair up and exchange books with a friend to complete the Observations section for each other. Talk over your observations before you return to your own book to respond to the Journal Prompt.

Let a week pass, perhaps two, and return for the next saint and her chapter. When you have worked through all the chapters, you will have a record of your journey, through your own eyes and the eyes of your friends, to read over again whenever you need company and encouragement.

Many of us have close friends who don't live near enough for regular visiting. But if you each have a copy of the book, you can meet on Facebook, Zoom, Skype, FaceTime, Google Hangouts, or any of the other online platforms with which we overcome the obstacles of time and space.

Find a way. May it be blessed!

# STONE

*Laura S. Jansson*

# *You Are Morwenna*

You are Morwenna. You live in a handmade hut at the top of an English cliff. The air tastes of salt spray and seaweed. The cries of choughs and kestrels wake you at dawn and soothe you at dusk. The wind billows and whistles around you, catching your breath and tossing it into your face. A wild sea batters the foot of your cliff, but you pray and seek peace in your hut, and you are not afraid.

The land behind you is lush and green but full of poverty and suffering. You are often there, breaking your solitude to visit the farmers and villagers. Their huts are small and handmade, just like yours, but their burdens are heavy, and they find no peace. Their children are hungry. Their clothes are threadbare. Their hearts are weary, seeking blindly for God.

You feel their sorrows crowding around you. You tend the sick and try to find food for the hungry. They thank you for your kindness, but you know that a full belly does not ease an anxious heart. In your quiet hut you find a comfort that you are not able to share with them.

One morning, you wake early with your face and hands pressed against the stone floor of your hut. You begin praying, as always, but the texture of the stone against your face and hands distracts you. You begin again, but a ray of early light finds its way through a crack in the door and shines on the stone by your hands.

The stone.

You pause in the middle of your prayer.

The stone.

You scramble up and open the door, gazing down through the mist to the rugged gray shore below. Stones of all sizes are heaped at the foot of the cliff, some bathed in the rush of seawater, some tumbled in piles along the beach. Stones to the north, stones to the south. Hundreds of stones, enough to build a cathedral, if only someone could bring them up to the green land above.

You know a path to the sea, a gravelly, twisting chain of footholds down the face of the cliff. You have traveled this path hundreds of times, and you no longer notice how your body leans this way and that to counter the uneven ground.

You reach the gray shingle, and the water sparkles under the rare gift of a clear sky at sunrise. You take one step, and there on the ground you see a smooth, rounded stone. It is large enough to use for building, but not so large that you are unable to lift it. Squatting down, you hoist it carefully and clasp it against your chest. You turn back to begin your journey up the face of the cliff. After a few steps, you realize you will need at least one hand free to make the climb safely. How will you carry the stone?

You pull up the hood of your thick cloak and rest the stone on your head like a crown. With one hand, you balance the stone. With the other, you steady yourself against the face of the cliff as you climb.

Your stone crown is hard and heavy. You feel the weight of it pressing down through the top of your head, bringing an ache to your neck and tightening your shoulders. You think of the hundreds of stones you will need to carry up this slippery path to

## Stone ~ Morwenna

build a church for the people at the top of the cliff. This will hurt.

But you think of the hungry children and the threadbare clothes. You think of the bowed heads and sorrowful eyes. You remember that you will never fit all the people into the bright, sweet solitude of your hut.

You settle the stone firmly on your woolen hood, brace your shoulders against the weight, and chant a prayer for strength as you march up the steep path.

When you reach the top, you walk a few paces away from the edge and lean forward, letting the stone drop to the earth. One journey, one stone.

You stretch your arms and shake your head to ease the muscles in your neck and back. You cross yourself and cross the stone with your shaking fingers. Then you entrust the stone to God and climb down the twisty path to the shore.

A second journey, a second stone. Then a third. The climb is slow and torturous. When darkness falls, you have carried only twenty stones to the top of the cliff. You return to your hut, and you are praying when you fall asleep on the stone floor.

In the morning, you begin again. You carry stones all day, and the craggy mound at the top is larger now. On the third day, you see children from the village staring with wide eyes as you come over the top of the cliff with a stone on your head. "For a church," you say, pointing to the piled stones. The children scamper away. You know that word will spread to everyone in the village by nightfall.

The stones are your life now. When you are awake, you are carrying stones. When you are not carrying stones, you are praying for sleep to heal your aching body. When you are asleep, you dream of a handmade church with a stone tower facing the sea.

One morning, the pain overwhelms you. Every sinew, every

bone seems compressed and drained of strength. When you reach the foot of the cliff, you wonder if your feet will carry you across the sand to gather the first stone. You have already taken all the stones near the path. You must walk farther and farther to collect new ones. Your journey is becoming infinite. You fear it will stretch you until you snap and crumble, like an old stone ground into sand.

You breathe the simple prayer, the prayer of three words only. Lord, have mercy.

Your eyes light on a good stone, a stone that looks like it would be at home in the wall of a handmade church with a tower facing the sea. You skirt the waves, crossing yourself. You lift the stone onto your shoulder, then up to its place on your head. The thick wool of your hood is worn as thin as a rose petal.

You think, as you cross the beach, that you will survive the journey. You think your strength will last, but your heart fails again as you struggle up the twisting path. For a moment, you feel the stone slipping from your grasp, and you almost tumble to your death on the sharp boulders below.

You stop. Slowly, you move the stone from your head to your shoulder, from your shoulder to the ground. You crouch beside the stone, and your body sinks into the curve of earth where the path meets the face of the cliff.

Your lips move. Your eyes close. Prayer and rest.

When you wake, you have not fallen. You are safe, and the stone is safe, and your strength has returned to you. You stand and raise your arms. You throw back your head, and a rare shaft of sunlight finds its way through the clouded air to touch your face.

You lift the stone up from the path and settle it like a crown on your head. You step forward, one hand guarding the stone, one hand guiding your journey up the dangerous, familiar path.

## Stone ⇒ Morwenna

When you reach the top, you add the stone to the pile and step back. The small pile has become a large pile, almost a mountain, almost a cathedral.

You cross yourself, and you cross the stones, throwing out your arms and leaping into the air so that this holy gesture will encompass the whole of your work—the stones, the earth, and the future that awaits them.

It is only as you are returning to the shore for another stone that you see the miracle. When you reach the place where you rested on the path, you find a spring of fresh water, rushing and singing as it escapes the rough earth.

ON THE LIFE OF THE SAINT

# Morwenna

SAINT MORWENNA LIVED in the British Isles in the fifth and sixth centuries; during the so-called Dark Ages, she was a ray of light in a land of long northern nights. The Orthodox prayer service devoted to all the saints of the British Isles calls St. Morwenna a holy virgin. She is also known as a hermitess and a teacher.

Morwenna is an Irish name meaning "sea maiden." The twelfth-century record in which she first appears names her as the daughter of the Irish-born King Brychan, himself a saint and the father of many saints. We can imagine she was raised on tales of St. Patrick, whose ministry to Ireland had taken place within her parents' living memory. It was in Wales that Brychan became king, and Morwenna seems to have regarded Wales as her homeland, later choosing to die where she could see its shores.

However, our holy mother is most beloved not in Ireland or Wales, but in Cornwall, on the southwesternmost peninsula of England. It's a land that has produced many saints; there are more saints in Cornwall, the old joke goes, than in heaven itself. Many among these saints were Morwenna's siblings, King Brychan's twenty-four children (twelve sons and twelve daughters). These could have been either his own offspring or spiritual children chosen for his great mission to the southwest and raised in his house.

Along with her sisters, Morwenna probably studied under a mother abbess, preparing to take on the role of evangelist. At a time when hardly anyone, least of all women, could read or write, she became knowledgeable about the Scriptures and herbalism, survival skills and animal husbandry, diplomacy and handicrafts. When she was ready, she crossed the channel to Cornwall.

She found there a scattered rural community of resourceful but impoverished people. They grew crops, raised livestock, hunted, foraged, and mined. They were skilled at weaving, pottery, dyeing, tanning, carving, and metalwork. They had a firm tribal social structure but were known to be hospitable and diplomatic negotiators on account of their contact with foreigners, for whom this peninsula was the first port of call. They held deep respect for creation, the cycles of nature, and spiritual forces. After the Romans invaded in AD 43, some aspects of Celtic religious practice (such as the Druidic Order and human sacrifice) were banned by the occupiers, but the people were still superstitious. They consulted the witches and wizards who lived off of devotees' offerings at sacred wells and standing stones. They held mass gatherings at burial sites, where there would be horse racing, dancing, divination, and animal sacrifice.

As Christians in this environment, the missionary children of Brychan must have leaned heavily on one another for encouragement. Saint Morwenna was closest to her brother St. Nectan, whom she summoned to give her communion at the time of her death. He was reputedly the oldest of Brychan's children and is the most revered. We have many more stories from his life than from Morwenna's, and there are places named after him in locations as widespread as Scotland and Brittany. Though this suggests he was quite a traveler, his primary mission field neighbored Morwenna's, just up the Cornish coast.

Morwenna and Nectan were not pioneering missionaries in Cornwall. Very early, the light of Christianity had been brought by traders and slaves navigating the long-established sea route from Phoenicia. Already in AD 208 Tertullian wrote that Christianity had reached parts of Britain yet inaccessible to the Roman army. Once the Roman occupation had run its course, Christianity had been the adopted religion of Rome (and therefore Roman Britain) for a century and a half.

By Morwenna's time, the Romans were gone. The last of them had departed in AD 410, leaving a power vacuum in their wake. Saxon migrants, whom the Celtic tribes regarded as barbarians, began to challenge their lands. The people of Cornwall turned for comfort back to their ancestral practices, and paganism took hold once more. Into this situation, the children of King Brychan came not to establish Christianity but to consolidate and strengthen the foundations laid by others so that the Faith in this place could endure a time of uncertainty. They came to bring Cornish Christianity back to life.

Despite her fine education and royal ties, evidently Morwenna was not afraid of getting her hands dirty. She first settled along what a document of 1296 calls "the ancient way," a path weaving along a windy clifftop. There, as she began to build a church with her own hands, a spring of water miraculously appeared. Residents of the area know the site of this spring, although it's now dry and inaccessible from the hillside. Other holy springs in the area still flow, including some dedicated to St. Nectan, and their water continues to be used for baptisms.

Just up the valley from her spring, the church Morwenna founded stands, and pilgrims still visit it today. It is known as the Anglican parish church of St. Morwenna and St. John the Baptist; Morwenstow, the village around it, also bears our saint's name. The church guidebook confirms that a reed-thatched Celtic chapel, dating to the sixth century, once stood on the present site. The current structure is newer, but parts still date to Norman times. On one of the interior walls a fresco has been uncovered that dates from around 1250. It shows St. Morwenna holding a book, perhaps the Gospels, and praying for a priest who kneels before her. It's as if she is offering her perpetual blessing to those who serve the community she founded.

Historically, Morwenna's church has offered people physical as well as spiritual protection. The bells rang from its tower not just to call people to prayer, but also to serve as an auditory lighthouse during stormy weather, alerting sailors that they were nearing the treacherous rocks below. Though the bell surely saved many lives, it could not save them all. During the nineteenth century, more than eighty shipwrecks were recorded in the area in one fifty-year period alone. Many of the unknown dead lie buried in Morwenna's churchyard.

According to one local historian, in addition to the church, St. Morwenna established a little monastic college nearby, perhaps with its own well, standing stone cross, livestock, infirmary, apothecary, gardens, library, and school. Often depicted with a group of children at her feet, or accompanied by a group of male and female disciples, our holy mother carefully taught and trained men, women, and children. One story holds that she became so renowned that she was summoned to teach the daughters of a British king. If, as some believe, King Arthur was a real person, he and Morwenna would have been contemporaries and likely would have met. On outings from his castle at Tintagel, twenty-five miles away, he would have taken advantage of the hospitality and spiritual counsel of surrounding monastic communities like hers. Even if the royal connections from Morwenna's earlier life remained, she was best known for her service to ordinary people, never neglecting to help them with their everyday needs.

Our saint fell asleep in the Lord in the early sixth century.

According to a fifteenth-century text, her relics rest under the floor of the church, where it's believed they remain to this day. No one knows their exact location, but an unmarked stone slab in the floor at the top of the nave may offer a clue. Its head is nearest the altar, signifying a particularly honorable burial. "I know that Morwenna lies here," confirmed the Rev. R. S. Hawker, an eccentric poet-pastor who served Morwenstow in the nineteenth century. "I have seen her, and she has told me as much; and at her feet ere long I hope to lay my old bones."

The community that worships in Morwenna's church has now dwindled to a remnant, but her efforts on their behalf were not in vain. By the end of the sixth century, according to her prayers and those of her missionary siblings, most of the southwestern peninsula was restored to Christian faith. Her feast is commemorated on July 8, and every year one local parish reenacts the events of her life at a festival in her honor. Cornish families still christen their daughters Morwenna. I even saw a bar bearing her name!

STEPPING FURTHER INTO THE STORY

# Water and Stone

I'VE COME ON a pilgrimage to the Cornish cliffs where St. Morwenna walked. As I stand at the edge of the green bluff, my knees weaken with the height and the climb. The hood of my coat whips my cheek; the clover at my feet stands nearly horizontal in the October wind. I look down to where my children and husband play on the beach below, the only people in the vast landscape.

Mostly, I see stone—stone in three forms. Swathes of dark orange sand settle into fields of grey sandstone boulders so massive they're hard to get perspective on, cut across with jagged rusty swords of layered shale pointing out to sea.

Over my shoulder, nestling into a valley carved by a stream, stands the church our mother Morwenna founded, part of the beach reconstituted in cruciform on the clifftop. Erected in the time when pagan practice dominated, these standing stones point not to the solstice sunrise but to the Light of the World. If any of the rocks remain that Morwenna herself carried up from the shore, they are now invisible, layered over with the renovation work of subsequent years. But fifteen centuries on, the community of faithful who worship here is still known by her name. If it weren't for her, they wouldn't be here.

Stone upon stone.

As well as stone I see water: the billowing vapor of water in the sky above the vast Atlantic Ocean, with the sunset beginning to dip golden in the west. Rising out of the sea several miles to the north is Lundy Island (named after its puffins in Old Norse), with a hint of the Welsh coast behind it. This is the treacherous shoreline of a resource-rich peninsula dangling alluringly into the Atlantic. It has wrecked as many ships as the Sirens, ever since the Phoenicians established their tin-trading route here a millennium and more before the time of Christ.

Water against stone.

This is the view on which Morwenna last closed her eyes. The air must have been clear that day. Tradition holds that, desiring to glimpse her dear native Wales once again before departing for her true home in the Kingdom, she had her brother St. Nectan prop her weakening body to face out across the water for a final look.

We can imagine them sitting quietly together, the reflected sea light playing on their faces, their eyes pensive as they think back on how far they've come since their missionary training together under King Brychan in the Welsh hills. Each with his or her own cell and turf and gifts, Morwenna and Nectan shared a calling to manifest the love of God to the people of Celtic Cornwall. Along the lanes, they encountered seekers scurrying to consult pagan oracles in their sacred groves. There where springs of water flowed from rock—wells still known by these saints' names today—they'd gathered little clutches of people eager to hear where the Living Water was to be found.

Water from stone.

They make a strange alchemy, stone and water. Somehow when light is added, we get gold. Burnt sienna, metallic waves, warm sand: the colors of Morwenna's cliffs are familiar to me from the city where I live, some four hours away. Oxford is also a place of golden stone, where not waves but spires gleam in the evening light behind the limestone walls of the colleges. These are the hallowed halls of learning, a shining fortress of human knowledge built up block upon block over the centuries. There you find gilded vellum, the brilliance of genius, the metallic flash of ancient church vessels.

But in Oxford as in Cornwall the waves continue to have their say. There too one can be dashed on the rock—shipwrecked on the steep cliffs of bookish pride, colonial hubris, reliance on human enterprise, and haughty forgetfulness of God. Even the gentle rain is a powerful force. Centuries of water falling from the sky have worn on the features of the stone gargoyles, columns, and monuments, slowly washing away what seemed so permanent.

Water strong as stone.

I remember in the final days before my fourth child was born, a dear friend pressed a gift into my hand. Her eyes sparkled as she watched me unfold the thin crinkly paper. Between its layers lay a plain grey pebble, the kind most beachcombers would pass over. But my friend had seen something special about it. Worn through its center was a smooth round hole that hinted quietly at a storied history of centuries spent tumbling with the sea. Through this hole she'd threaded a string, making of this ordinary object a piece of jewelry.

Water in conversation with stone.

Not everyone would treasure a holey pebble as a present, but this friend and I understood each other. We both have homes decorated with finds from our latest walks: abandoned wasps' nests, barnacles, feathers, driftwood, animal bones, and lacy leaves. Also, this friend knew a thing or two about having babies. Not only had she birthed several children of her own (I'd seen her do it), but as a midwife she had witnessed scores of other women's babies enter the world. I was ready to listen to what she wanted to tell me.

She intended, she said, that I should wear the necklace during my coming labor. It would remind me that I would become as strong as rock in order to give birth. I would need to gather my full courage to withstand the buffeting of the storm. However, I must also be soft enough to be porous. Like the stone with the hole, I would let the great forces of nature pass through me, not fighting against but yielding to them. If I could find a way to do this, the waves of my contractions would not be my undoing. They would not toss me, smash me, destroy me. Instead, like water navigating the pebble, they would flow through, reshaping me into something new: something more rounded, perhaps—something less self-contained and more wide open. Something like the mother I would need to be.

Water reforming stone.

When my labor started a couple of weeks later, I found myself fidgeting with this gifted necklace. With every contraction that rolled onto my shore, my big belly grew rock-hard, and my strength eroded a little more. Stronger and stronger they came, returning over and over with just a few moments' rest in between. As the night wore on, I began to wear thin with the pain, the exertion, the exhaustion. Just before daybreak I began to feel I had nothing left. I was broken. I could not continue under my own strength.

As a doula experienced in reading the signposts of childbirth, I watch for this point in every labor. For there seems to be a pattern: just at the moment a laboring woman starts to give up hope that her child will ever be born, a tide of energy bursts upon her, bearing the baby aground.

I have seen this many times. "I'm not doing this anymore. I'm done," a woman will say, sweaty, writhing sideways to look me in the face. "No, really, I can't." And then the next contraction sweeps in, bringing the first urge to bear down. She is doing it. No one can take this cup from her.

But she is right, in an important way. "I'm done" is an expression of the dawning realization that her own strength is insufficient for the monumental task of bringing a new human being out through her body and into the world. This is one occasion when she cannot slide by with the usual recipe of planning, willpower, and micromanagement. Nothing she can do will get this baby born. She must now stand aside and let it happen in her.

Yet her admission of weakness itself unlocks a new power. As she gets out of the way, a mightier force can complete its work. She does go on, not by her own strength but by the creative power of God moving in her.

At the birth of a child, an esoteric theological saying leaps off the page of the Scriptures to manifest itself before the very eyes of those privileged to be present. With sinews and bones and fluids and groans, we see: "When I am weak, then I am strong."

Sure enough, just a few minutes after I conceded, my daughter was born.

For all of us, male or female, parent or not, that's what it's often like, isn't it? It's at the end of our own tether that the miracle happens. It is in our greatest weakness that God's strength is known. It's when we decrease that He can increase. It's in losing our life that we find it.

To put it another way: it's in the spot where St. Morwenna falls down, exhausted, that her spring rises up. It's when the people of God curse Moses in the wilderness and wish themselves back in Egypt that they hear the crack of the staff, the gush of water through the rock. It's when God Himself is spat upon and mocked and bleeding and dead that the glorious Resurrection is ushered in.

We women pride ourselves on our strength. We want to show the world that we can do what we set our minds to. That we are worthy of the equality society says it accords to us. That our foremothers' sacrifices on our behalf have not been in vain. That we are busy, accomplished, ambitious, and self-reliant enough to count.

Stone.

Indeed, certain times call for strength. We can rise with fierce womanly love to defend those who cannot protect themselves. Sometimes we muster great bravery to break out of a prison of abuse. Or, with every ounce of determination, we goad ourselves to complete an impossible task. For a good cause, we grit our teeth, push through the pain, and only stop to note the blood afterward. Much to our credit, we women really know how to set our faces like flint.

But other occasions make us acutely conscious of how vulnerable we are to the elements. The repetition of our daily tasks, like the return of waves on the rocks, grinds us down. Our imperfections—the pits and dents and cracks roughhewn by the ocean—haunt us. The pain of life reaches us through new holes that open up right at the center of our hearts. Sometimes we are worn so thin that it feels like only the most fragile of layers remains to hold us together.

We do well to remember that our true strength lies in being permeable. Only stone that can be worked is used for monuments. We are not weaker but stronger when we let the healing love of God and of others flow in. Our pain need not erode us entirely but can instead soften, smooth, and shape us for a new purpose. The swirling water can dissolve a heart of stone into a heart of flesh.

"You also, as living stones, are being built up a spiritual house," writes St. Peter (1 Pet. 2:5). Let us be stones. But let us be porous stones, because God does not force His way into a rocky fortress; rather, He seeps in through the worn places.

If we are stones that have been struck, let us pour forth the water of life. If we are dry stones in the desert, let us become bread, the body of Christ with which He feeds the world. If we are small, smooth river stones, let us fell the giant. If we are stones raised in judgment, let us be dropped back onto the dusty ground. If we are stones eroded, let us become a cave where Christ can be born. If we are big rounded stones, let us be rolled away from tombs to reveal the Resurrection. If we are quirky and misshapen stones like those St. Morwenna chose on the beach, let us be slotted up against the contours of others to build the Church.

PERSONAL SURVEY

# My Stones, My Cliff, My Church

*The sacrifices of God are a broken spirit,*
*A broken and contrite heart—*
*These, O God, You will not despise.*
*—Psalm 50/51:17*

What are the waves that have tumbled and formed you? The painful experiences of your life that have contributed to who you are?

_____

_____

_____

_____

The hole in the pebble Laura's friend gave to her allowed it to be made into a necklace. Which of your irregularities or wounds can be used to make you a gift to others?

_____

_____

_____

What is the most perilous coastline in your spiritual landscape? Against which stone cliffs does your ship most often run aground?

*Stone ~ Morwenna*

When a stone wall is built, the mason selects suitable stones and leaves others aside. As you build a home for God in your heart, are there any stones that don't belong—any habits or relationships that don't help you to create a stable, beautiful, and durable temple?

Where St. Morwenna rested from her labors, a spring rose up, refreshing with clear cold water not only the saint but also her whole community. Where in your life do you need a fruitful and restorative rest?

When your life comes to a close and you prop yourself up to look over the landscape of your days, what do you hope to have built?

OBSERVATIONS FROM A FRIEND

# Building a Wall Together

Imagine yourself and your discussion partner as stones in the wall of the Church of God, each uniquely shaped and contributing her own special beauty and function to the temple. How would you describe the contours of your partner's gifts?

As part of the temple's walls, your partner may not be able to see the vital ways in which she is supporting others. How do you see her life currently being used for the edification of the Church?

Morwenna labored with her hands to build the church of Morwenstow, but she and Nectan labored together to build the Church of Cornwall. How can the two of you work together to build Christ's Church in your own time and place?

"It is no longer I who live, but Christ lives in me" (Gal. 2:20). Share with your partner a story from your own life when God's power was revealed precisely at the point where your own abilities had been exhausted. Where has God brought your life back to life?

JOURNAL PROMPT

# Between the Rock and the Hard Place, a Wellspring of Joy

"MY STRENGTH IS made perfect in weakness" (2 Cor. 12:9), our Lord reassures St. Paul.

We see this truth in St. Morwenna, who expends her life to bring joy to the people of Cornwall, symbolized by the springing forth of a water source in the cliffside spot where her strength was spent.

We see it also in the cave where Christ is born. The Almighty expresses the fullness of His love in the person of Jesus, who comes as a tiny baby in a mucky stable to share every corner of human life, even our vulnerability and pain.

We see it throughout our Lord's ministry, where He bends down to the stone floor to wash a tax collector's feet and allows His own feet to be cleaned by a prostitute. He is the stone the builders rejected, at home not among the wealthy and the noble but among ordinary people like us.

We see it in His rocky Tomb, where the salvation of the world takes place through a criminal's death. The Light of the World descends into Hades, enlightening the souls overshadowed by darkness.

We may see it in our own lives, too, where in our meager, sinful, needy, and stony hearts, a spring of water wells up to eternal life. Strength made perfect in weakness: what does this mean in your life?

*Stone* ⌒ *Morwenna*

# SONG

*Georgia Briggs*

# You Are Kassiani

You are Kassiani, and you see the world through a sharp, pure light. Your ears and your mind are trained to discern melody, and your skillful fingers write it plainly. You are brave, but you are not always patient.

This is the quiet hour, the midafternoon peace of a warm day when the nuns in your monastery are occupied with tasks they can accomplish without your supervision. You have withdrawn to your cell with parchment, pen, and ink. A small table is there, empty of everything but what you bring to it. As you write, your lips move slightly and your breathing changes, as if you are chanting the music you hear in your solitude.

It is a difficult song. You are thinking deeply as you write, and your thoughts are like the shadows of leaves, wavering over the grass below a windswept tree. Patches of brightness, patches of darkness, changing swiftly.

*The woman who had fallen into many sins recognizes Thy Godhead, O Lord. She takes upon herself the duty of a myrrh-bearer and makes ready the myrrh of mourning, before Thy entombment.*

The scent of myrrh rises from the page—perhaps in fact, perhaps in memory. It is so familiar to you, and you are so deeply engaged in your song, that you scarcely notice it.

*Woe to me! saith she, for my night is an ecstasy of excess, gloomy and moonless, and full of sinful desire.*

The scent fades as you hesitate over the words. The flushed face of the sinful woman is visible in your mind—her eyes reddened, the lashes clinging together in peaks from so much weeping, her hands moving nervously around her face, brushing away strands of hair and dripping tears. You know that her heart is full. You close your eyes for her, peering into the dark space where she finds herself. Her weakness seems powerful to her, like an angry strength that will succeed in crushing her.

*Receive the sources of my tears, O Thou who dost gather into clouds the water of the sea; in Thine ineffable condescension, deign to bend down Thyself to me and to the lamentations of my heart, O Thou who didst spread out the heavens.*

The clouds, the water of the sea, the great Strength stooping into the human realm to heal the sources of her tears—the images pour through you into the words, into the melody, until a sound outside of you dams the stream abruptly.

You lift your head, listening. The song inside you is silent. You feel the air moving through your open window. You see the table in front of you again, the swift, light strokes of ink on parchment that moments before were playing aloud as you created them.

Someone is coming. You hear sounds in the monastery courtyard beyond your window. They are not the sounds of nuns at work, not prayers or bells. The world has come through your gates. You breathe in sharply. You know who is there.

You push the table away. You have dropped completely out of the song you were writing. Time is fluid in the monastery. It can melt away from you in an instant, and you travel wherever the spirit wills.

YOUR PLAIN BLACK ROBE TRANSFORMS to vivid silk, your hair is laced with scent and ribbon, your eyes are bright but wary. You are the most beautiful woman in the imperial court, a contestant in the bride show, chosen for review by the dowager empress. The young Emperor Theophilus stands before you, and you know that you are both powerful and powerless.

You make your face still and calm. You meet his eyes, but you pray fervently and silently.

There is something about him. You know that he also is powerful—powerless before God, no doubt—but in this room, on this earth, he is powerful. You watch him as he pauses, as he walks toward you, as he hefts the golden apple resting in his right hand. Beside you, your friend Theodora gazes down at her own hands, tightly folded. Theophilus takes one more step, and now you are no more than an arm's length apart.

Low-voiced conversations cease in every corner. The dowager empress stares at you intently. Theophilus stares at you also, but his gaze is not like hers.

"Through a woman came the baser things." He presses words deliberately into the silence.

*Eve. He is challenging me with Eve.* You smile. This is easily answered.

"And through a woman came the better things," you reply bravely. *Most Holy Theotokos, save us.*

His eyes widen, his brows lift. You hear a quick breath, his perhaps, or the ripple of nervous surprise around the attentive room.

Theodora lifts her eyes shyly, and Theophilus turns to her. The golden apple is lost to you. Relief surges behind your composure. You are saved for the life you will choose for yourself. But no one will forget that once, for a few shimmering seconds, you were nearly an empress.

YOU HAVE STOOD HERE ONLY a few seconds, frozen next to your half-finished song as the voices of Theophilus and his retinue grow louder outside your window. Time is fluid. So much can be compressed into so little of it.

You dip the pen quickly in ink, begging just one fragment more of the song before Theophilus finds you. You know that he has come to the monastery for only one purpose.

But the song. The words are coming to you again. No time to sit down, so you steady the parchment with one hand and lean over it breathlessly.

*I will fervently embrace Thy sacred feet, and wipe them again with the tresses of the hair of my head—*

You drop the pen. You can hear his footsteps in the corridor, swift and purposeful.

Behind you is a closet. You wrench open the wooden door and plunge inside, closing yourself in as silently as you can. You try to control your breathing. It sounds loud to you in the darkness.

You hear a knock, then his voice calling your name, a pause, and the door of your cell opening and his footsteps entering. Nothing separates you from Emperor Theophilus but a handmade wooden door.

"Kassiani?"

He is almost panting. Perhaps he does not move so quickly down the corridors of his palace.

"Kassiani?"

You hear him cross the small room. He must be near the window or by the table.

"You were here." His voice is lower now, accepting that he is probably talking to himself. You hear the sound of fingers brushing parchment, of a pen rolling to one side. "What have you been writing, I wonder?"

You bite your lip. The song is precious to you, only half written. You pray for the parchment under his hand. *Grant this, O Lord.*

You are still, and he is still. You hold your breath. Will he hear you? Will he find you?

You hear the small, crisp sounds of a pen at work. He is writing, but only briefly.

Silence again. A soft sound, as if something has brushed against the parchment on your table. His fingers?

The door closes firmly behind him, and you hear his footsteps receding down the corridor.

Emperor Theophilus is gone.

You count slowly to one hundred as a precaution. He does not return. You fling open the door and rush to your table.

Your eyes scramble over the words you have written: I will fervently embrace Thy sacred feet, and wipe them again with the tresses of the hair of my head—

What is this? Below your own writing, you see his, thick and dark as if he leaned heavily on the pen.

*Those feet at whose sound Eve hid herself for fear when she heard Thee walking in Paradise in the cool of the day,* he has written.

Eve again. A woman hiding in Paradise. Did he know that you were hiding also, behind him in the closet? *Most Holy Theotokos, save us.*

You drop to your knees by the table, and your prayers rise within you as the pen races.

*O my Savior and soul-Saver, who can trace out the multitude of my sins, and the abysses of Thy judgment? Do not disregard me Thy servant, O Thou whose mercy is boundless.*

ON THE LIFE OF THE SAINT

# *Kassiani*

FROM HER YOUTH, Saint Kassiani was outspoken and scholarly. Although most Byzantine women of her class had some education, Kassiani pursued academic knowledge and spiritual understanding to a degree surpassing any requirement for an accomplished young lady to find a good husband. She was known even as a teenager for her poetry, songs, and essays. Saint Theodore the Studite himself was her mentor and thought highly of her abilities. In one letter to her he wrote, "Once more your Decorum has expressed to us things so wise and understanding that it is right for me to be astonished and give thanks to the Lord when I see such knowledge in a maiden lately sprung. . . . The fair form of your discourse has far more beauty than a mere specious prettiness."\*

Not that she lacked physical beauty. The young Kassiani was exceptionally lovely, and as the story goes, she was in love with the young emperor-to-be, Theophilus, when his mother invited her to compete in the bride-show to be his wife. The only problem was the clash of their beliefs; Theophilus would try to rid the empire of icons, while Kassiani believed strongly that icons had an important place in the Church.

It must have been tempting for Kassiani to see the man she admired holding out the apple that signified her victory. He was

---

\* Susan Arida, "The Theological Voice of St. Kassiani," *The Church Across Time*. The Wheel, 2017. www.wheeljournal.com

an iconoclast, she an iconodule. He was so different from her, yet she was attracted to him.

"From a woman came the baser things," he said, offering her the fruit.

I wonder if she had her moment of clarity when she saw him, offering her power and pleasure with a piece of fruit as Satan had once tempted Eve.

"And from a woman came the better things," she replied.

What an amazing response. By adding to his belittling words, she turned his insult easily into a summary of our identities as women—the gender through whom sin was introduced to the world and through whom God Himself was born into the world. Yes, she essentially said. But also.

Theophilus was taken aback by her outspokenness and chose Theodora, a meeker girl, for his bride. Even in this he underestimated women, for Theodora secretly disobeyed him and brought up their children to venerate icons.* She outlived her husband and later called the leaders of the Church to hold the Seventh Ecumenical Council, which affirmed the position of icons as windows to heaven and thus worthy of honor, but not worship.

I love the contrast between the two women. Saint Kassiani and St. Theodora show us that Christianity can be lived out faithfully by both the meek and the valiant. Theodora persevered in secret faithfulness. Kassiani spoke out through her writings. She became a nun and eventually founded her own monastery, where Theophilus sought her out once more in the episode recounted in this book.

While St. Kassiani was writing her most famous *Hymn of the*

---

\* John Sanidopoulos, "Saint Kassiani the Hymnographer," Mystagogy Resource Center, September 7, 2015. https://www.johnsanidopoulos.com/2015/09/saint-kassiani-hymnographer.html

*Penitent Woman*, she heard that Theophilus had come to the monastery, and she avoided him by hiding in the closet. She had just written the words, "I shall kiss Thine immaculate feet, and wipe them with the tresses of my head."

It is most telling and fascinating that she hid. Was she afraid Theophilus would take her by force, or was she perhaps overcome by her feelings? Her uncharacteristic avoidance seems like good evidence that she'd once loved him.

Theophilus came into the room and, finding her gone, read what she had written. He added, "those feet at whose sound Eve hid herself for fear when she heard Thee walking in Paradise in the cool of the day."

Saint Kassiani came out from her hiding place after he left and evidently liked the line, as it is still in the song. Once again she accepted his words and used them to create an expression of greater truth. The hymn is a beautiful image of humanity's—and especially woman's—relationship with God.

Saint Kassiani went on to write numerous other works, focusing often on the parallels between Eve and the Mother of God. She composed many verses on the lives of female saints. Her path diverged from the emperor's as she spoke out vehemently against iconoclasm, to the point of incurring persecution and even public whippings.

Although Theophilus's intentions in visiting the monastery are unclear, his line highlighting woman's shame before God provided Kassiani with the beginning of the most beautiful parallel in her song, just as his insult at the bride-show gave her the opportunity to express her greater wisdom. She didn't erase his criticism but worked it into her song to give a fuller picture of the truth. Yes, we have fallen. Yes, we have done wrong. Yes, we are the daughters of Eve. But also. Look at the beauty of Christ's mercy mingling with our tears. Look at how He transforms us through repentance and love.

Because of her bravery and dedication to speaking the truth, St. Kassiani remained free of Theophilus's control. She devoted the remainder of her life to God in the monastery she founded. Her songs are still sung during Holy Week in churches to this day.

STEPPING FURTHER INTO THE STORY

# The Better Things

SAINT KASSIANI'S ICON hangs in the southern transept of our church, standing behind the choir members and watching us as we sing. Her head is tilted, her expression one of concentration, as though she is trying to decide if a certain alto is a little off-key. The scroll in her hands bears the opening words of her most famous hymn, which we sing every year on Holy Wednesday.

*The woman had fallen into many sins, O Lord,*
*but when she perceived Thy divinity,*
*she joined the ranks of the myrrh-bearing women.*
*In tears she brought Thee myrrh*
*before Thy burial;*
*she cried, "Woe is me! For I have lived in the night of licentiousness,*
*shrouded in the dark and moonless love of sin.*
*But accept the fountain of my tears,*
*Thou who didst scatter the waters into clouds!*
*Bow down Thine ear to the sighings of my heart . . ."*

In our parish, the *Hymn of the Penitent Woman* is sung by a man. There's a simple reason for this: when our choir began singing more complicated hymns, this singer was the only one familiar with the Byzantine melody. His voice is so beautiful that he's performed it ever since, with the female choristers providing harmony.

Since the tradition was established before I came to the church, I asked the choir director why St. Kassiani's hymn was not sung by a woman.

"Why would you ask that?" he said, taken aback.

"Because . . . it was written by a woman and from a woman's point of view?" I answered. I hoped he didn't think I wanted to sing it. My voice would crack on the high notes, and he knew that. But there are some sopranos in the choir who surely could do it.

The director told me about the singer being the only one who knew the melody at the beginning. "And besides," he added, "the real point of the song is that we are all the woman weeping at Christ's feet, whether we are male or female, since we have all fallen and come back to repent."

It's true. It's absolutely true.

But here's the hard thing—the thing that I as a twenty-first-century Orthodox woman have to deal with on a daily basis, the thing that I have so much trouble with, the thing that St. Kassiani managed to overcome . . .

We are always singing backup, aren't we?

Women often serve less glamorous roles in the Church. We are the ones rushing out of the Liturgy to pull spanikopitas out of the oven. We are the ones waiting outside the door to the altar for a boy to go get the keys to the church hall. We are the ones standing veiled and quiet while our husbands read the epistle. I hear the rich tenor voices singing the men's-only opening to *Eis Polla Eti Despota,* and beside me another alto sings quietly an octave below because she wants to be a part of it.

It's hard to write these things, because I love Orthodoxy. I love my priest, my choir director, and most of all my husband, who spends every Sunday holding our two-year-old so that I can sing.

I don't want anyone to think I'm angry or unappreciative of the hard work men do in the Church.

But can we admit that it's still hard?

At least I admire and respect the men in authority over me. There are plenty of less fortunate women. I think of St. Kassiani, a young poet and songwriter with a pen sharper than a sword, standing in a line of dolled-up women for a spoiled young prince to judge, and I feel the frustration welling up inside me.

To live the Christian life, Christ tells us, is to be humble. To be the last. To be the least. To be a servant. But how is it fair if Kassiani is asked to be humbled and Theophilus is not?

What if I am asked to be the lesser while another isn't? If everyone must be self-deprecating and quiet, then fine, but why just me?

And now I've switched to the singular pronoun, me, because this is where I drop the act. In my heart of hearts, it doesn't bother me that women and men have different roles in the Church, or what reasons God has for that.

This is the real struggle inside me—that I am asked to play a humbler role when I want the role that's most recognized and most appreciated. I am theoretically fine with Christ telling everyone that the first shall be last and the last shall be first. I applaud His command to humble ourselves and wash each other's feet. Except when I'm the one asked to do so.

And I bet you have felt the same way at one time or another.

You see the challenge presented to women, the challenge presented to St. Kassiani when Theophilus offered her the apple.

"From woman came the baser things," said the spoiled young emperor, looking down his nose at her.

It's important to understand that Theophilus in this moment was not representing the male gender or the patriarchy. He was a type of Satan, offering Eve the fruit all over again. Here. Be empowered through abasement. Be the Empress of All, by taking it at the price of your conscience.

Saint Kassiani could have denied Theophilus's insult and argued with him, shaming him in front of the crowd with her superior wit. Or she could have lowered herself and pandered to his ego and lust, making some kind of suggestive comment on how "bad" she could be, winning the contest and gaining power by becoming empress.

Instead she accepted his insult and tempered it with truth. "And from Woman came the better things."

He had tempted her with Eve, and she answered him with the Theotokos.

Saint Kassiani understood that the Virgin Mary is the true picture of women's place in Christianity. Kassiani's writings often focused on the two archetypes women must choose between—Eve and the Mother of God. It's the underlying theme of the *Hymn of the Penitent Woman*, even though the Theotokos is never mentioned in the song by name. The woman who had fallen into many sins has run away from God, like Eve, but now anoints His feet with her tears and wipes them with her hair. She joins the ranks of the myrrh-bearers—the sisters and Mother of Christ. The ones who loved Him so much that they followed Him even after He died.

Only by looking at the Theotokos can we see how beloved and important we are to God. She is the woman who was never a priest, but sits enthroned above every altar. She never read a Gospel in church, but gave birth to the Word Himself. Her glory surpasses any other saint's because of her love, humility, and obedience.

Saint Kassiani made her own choice between Eve and the Theotokos. She rejected the apple and took up a veil instead of a crown, becoming a mother of many spiritual daughters. And like the Mother of God, St. Kassiani was lifted up and honored. Her veil became her crown, as the songs she wrote in the monastery became some of the most beloved hymns of Orthodoxy.

I am a woman. I am an alto. I am a poor sight-reader, I'm constantly short of breath when I sing, and every other week I'm trying to make it through the cherubic hymn with a two-year-old who's whining for a snack. These things are frustrating to me. If I could be the amazing tenor who carries the choir through the whole service, I would.

But maybe it's for the salvation of my soul that I don't try to take an apple that isn't meant for me. The Mother of God was a woman, entrusted to the keeping of men, and probably exhausted from lugging around the toddler who would bring salvation to the world. Maybe singing backup is the more glorious song, in the end.

Saint Kassiani's choice between Eve and the Theotokos is mine to make, and yours to make as well. We make the choice every day when we act in faith that the least of us shall be great in the Kingdom of God. Our paths may look different; some of us may lay aside the talents we enjoy to take care of the families God gave us, while others of us may lay aside our desire for family to do the work we are called to do. Either way we are asked to give up our own ideal for our lives—to die to ourselves—and let Christ be our families and our passion.

"Let it be unto me according to Your will," we choose to say.

And then from us will come the better things.

PERSONAL SURVEY

# Turning Down the Apple

In which areas of your life is it especially hard to take a humble role?

If there is an apple of temptation in your life, what do you think it is?

Saint Kassiani found a way to use her voice and her gifts for God's glory and not her own. How could you do this in your situation?

Who are some women in your life who have truly become types of the Theotokos? How have you seen her in their actions?

When do you find it hardest to accept someone's criticism?

When do you find it hardest to remember your worth?

When was a time you fled from God, like Eve in the Garden?

Do you remember a moment when you sat down and wept at Christ's feet? What did this look like for you?

How can you take a humble role in the future while remembering your own worth?

OBSERVATIONS FROM A FRIEND

# *Beautiful Struggle*

Speak with your friend about some areas in your lives where you struggle to live like the Theotokos instead of like Eve. How are your challenges similar to each other's?

Are there some areas—in family or career—where your challenges are opposite? Do you ever struggle to appreciate the work and sacrifices of others?

How do you think you can encourage and support each other in areas where you feel tired and frustrated?

What are some rewards you and your friend have experienced when you have followed the examples of St. Kassiani and the Theotokos?

*Song ❧ Kassiani*

Part of St. Kassiani's lasting contribution to the Church was the beauty of her songs. How do you see your friend bringing beauty and holiness to those around her, even in small ways that often go unnoticed?

JOURNAL PROMPT

# The Song of Your Life

*I will sing to the LORD as long as I live; I will sing praise to my God while I have being.*
—Psalm 104:33

THIS IS YOUR chance to write your song, just as St. Kassiani did centuries ago. Start by quieting yourself. Let go of all your daily cares—the deadlines, the dishes, the drama—and bring your awareness once again to your place before God. You are both Eve and the penitent woman. You are a type of them both, and now in writing you become a type of St. Kassiani.

Write to God whatever is on your heart and mind. Write without judging or editing your words, so they can flow freely. Remember, this is for you and God. There's no need to be anything but honest.

When you find your voice, leave behind your immediate feelings and write the song of your life. Where did you begin, and how has God transformed you? How have you run from Him, and what has brought you back to His feet? Write as literally or symbolically as you like, but don't stop until your song is on paper.

---------------------------------------------------
---------------------------------------------------
---------------------------------------------------
---------------------------------------------------
---------------------------------------------------

*Song* ❧ *Kassiani*

# LEAF

*Molly Sabourin*

# *You Are Ia*

YOU ARE IA, running down the stony path to the sea. Mist floats and swirls around you, the uneven ground tilts and dips beneath your flying feet. You hear your cloak flapping and seabirds calling in the gray dawn. You are late.

Your heart pounds with effort. This is the day. Fingar and Piala have arranged a ship. The Christians will cross the Irish Sea to Cornwall, and you will be with them, bringing the words of Christ on your lips and the joy of Him in your heart.

You hardly slept. Your mind was full of stories, plans, instructions, and you tossed and twisted in your blanket until you wondered if you would ever sleep again. Then you slept, suddenly and deeply, and when you woke, the others had gone ahead of you.

You are closer now. Your breath is short, and your mind is seething. Small stones slip out from under your feet and roll across the path. You slow to a rapid walk. Your arms flail, tangling in your billowing cloak. The ground is steep here, and the wind is stronger. Saltwater scent stings your nostrils, and you hear waves rushing against the shingle ahead.

Your eyes roam the earth, watching for footholds. You've been carrying your staff, moving too quickly to use it, but now you need it to keep your balance. You wonder suddenly if you are more excited or frightened. You are absorbed in your journeying, and you do not look ahead until you are safely on the beach.

No one is here.

Around you, everything is in motion. A brisk wind banishes the mist. The surf rolls and crashes. Birds swoop. Your clothes ripple and flap. Only you are still, completely still except for your head, turning in every direction, seeking frantically for people you know should be here.

No one. Not Fingar or Piala. Not anyone.

Your hair whips your face like an urgent red banner. You climb a rough brown boulder, and your eyes race to the horizon. A ship is slipping away from you, over the Irish Sea to Cornwall. They have gone without you.

"No! Wait for me!"

You plunge off the boulder and run a few steps along the sea, calling, but you know they are far beyond the reach of your voice.

You crumple up like a sail emptying as the wind turns elsewhere. How could they leave you? Did no one think to waken you? Did no one say, "We must bring Ia! Please wait while I look for her"?

Could not God have wakened you if He truly meant you to bring His light to Cornwall?

You are young. You feel foolish. Shame and grief fill your throat.

You crouch by the water's edge, leaning on your staff. The hard, knotty wood against the palm of your hand recalls the sunny afternoon at the forest's edge when you cut a tree branch and painstakingly stripped away the twigs and bark, telling yourself that you would need this staff for walking when you became a missionary to Cornwall. You were excited, confident.

Now you are alone with your staff, abandoned at the brink.

Your eyes are salty. You blink to clear them. In a few minutes, you will have to trudge back to the village and explain to the curious and scornful that you weren't chosen after all.

You close your eyes tight and listen to the water lapping the sand at your feet. Come and go, come and go. This water could bring you to Cornwall, if only you had a boat.

You open your eyes. A tiny green leaf bobs on the water in front of you. Like a prism, the green leaf and the silver-gray water seem to gather and scatter every color—emerald, ruby, sapphire, diamond. A sparkling droplet, no bigger than a tear, rolls gently on the surface of the leaf.

Come and go, come and go. The leaf rocks, and the motion soothes and fascinates you. Everything fades away from the leaf—the sounds and scents around you, the turmoil inside you. The leaf floats, the teardrop rides. Your eyes follow it. Come and go, come and go.

Almost involuntarily, you lift your staff and reach out, tapping the leaf gently. The leaf rocks a little, like a boat whisking past an eddy in the water. You tap it again, and still the leaf floats.

Suddenly, urgently, you know the leaf is important. As the feeling swells in your heart, the leaf swells on the water. For several seconds, you wonder if you are dreaming dreams and seeing visions. It is a real leaf. How can it be growing?

But it is growing. *They that go down to the sea in ships, that do business in great waters; These see the works of the* LORD, *and His wonders in the deep.*

The leaf is growing, and your joy is growing with it, trembling, wavering, rising up like the brightening waves. Come and go, come and go!

You know now. You know that the leaf is your boat, and you know that you are chosen after all. Grasping your staff in your right hand and your billowing travel cloak in your left, you jump lightly across the breaking foam onto the green leaf. You feel the sinewy fibers hardening under your feet. It is time.

You turn your face eastward, to Cornwall and your mission. The breeze quickens around you, and the leaf bounds forward as if it carried a strong mast and well-made sails. The swift waters sing around your green leaf.

"I am coming!" you shout, as you catch a glimpse of the wooden ship gliding along the approaching horizon. The distance closes between you and the boat you missed this morning. Time seems to close with it, and you pass from late to early as the bright green stem passes the sturdy brown prow.

"I am coming!" you shout again, and you wave your hands in the air, dancing, calling out to your fellow missionaries. You see them rush to the rails of their boat. You see them pointing at your magnificent leaf. Their words are tossed away on the wind of your passing, but you see shock and wonder on their faces.

As you pass the wooden boat, your eyes seek the horizon again, and you see the Cornish coast approaching. It looks like a large, mossy rock, all jagged cliffs with green grass above and gold-gray sand below.

You understand, suddenly, that you will be first on this new shore. Your leaf will come up through the low surf, and you will hear it brush over the sand. It will stop moving, and you will be in Cornwall. You will be a real missionary from the moment your feet touch dry ground.

"Am I frightened?" you ask yourself, squeezing your hands tightly around your staff. Time is folding up quickly now. Your mission is tumbling out of the future into the near present.

For several seconds, the forward motion feels like panic, feels like rushing, feels like something you are unprepared to meet.

But the leaf never pauses. It carries you smoothly along the crest

*Leaf & Ia*

of the Irish Sea, and the sight of your two plain-shod feet standing so safely on a mysterious green leaf brings you great peace. If a girl who was late to her calling can cross the sea on a leaf, she has no need to fear any place where it brings her.

You are chosen. You cannot be unchosen now. You have been given a miracle. After that, there can be nothing left to fear.

ON THE LIFE OF THE SAINT

# *Ia*

SAINT IA, SOMETIMES referred to as Eia, Hia, or Hya, lived during the fifth or sixth century and is believed to have been the daughter of an Irish chief, as well as a disciple of St. Piala and St. Fingar. Legend has it that Ia intended to accompany Ss. Fingar, Piala, and 777 of their companions on an evangelistic journey from her native Ireland to Cornwall, but when she arrived on the seashore to catch the ship, she discovered that they had left without her. They felt she was too young to endure the arduous trip.

Ia was devastated and beyond disappointed to have been abandoned and deemed too fragile to carry out the mission God had placed on her heart. She wept and prayed, and as she prayed she became aware of a tiny leaf floating on the surface of the water. When she reached out and touched it with her staff, the little leaf began to grow, and grow, and keep on growing until it was large enough for her to climb onto. Ia trusted that this miracle was a gift from God and allowed the leaf to swiftly carry her across the sea from Ireland to Cornwall, where she safely landed ahead of the ship she'd missed that morning.

Not much is known for certain about her adventures in Cornwall thereafter, but it is believed St. Ia worked tirelessly for many years there building churches and spreading the gospel. Most of the Christians who made a home for themselves in St. Ia's mission were martyred by a pagan ruler, but Ia herself escaped martyrdom at that time and continued her evangelistic work, earning the respect of a local lord named Dinan, who built a church for Ia in St. Ives Bay at her request.

Another legend says that St. Ia built a small cell for herself in Cornwall where she would retreat to pray in solitude. Eventually, however, Ia too would face martyrdom. The exact date of her martyrdom is uncertain, but St. Ia is venerated as one of the evangelizers of Cornwall and as the first recorded female martyr on British land. A church was built over her grave.

Saint Ia is commemorated by the Church on February 3.

STEPPING FURTHER INTO THE STORY

# A Miraculous Voyage

ONE OF MY kids' favorite books when they were little was a Sesame Street collection of fables I picked up at a thrift store in Chicago. One particular fable they wanted me to read over and over again was about a king who had accidentally dropped his gold down a small opening in the castle floor. The wisest and strongest people in his kingdom were unable to rescue his treasure, but a small, shy boy approached the agitated king and offered to be of service. With all eyes upon him, that little boy got down on his belly and slowly lowered his tiny, slender arm into the crevice. A few seconds later, he pulled forth the gold, and the king was overjoyed! My kids were captivated by the notion that everyone has a very specific role they are meant to play on this earth.

Though I am no longer small or young, I too am encouraged by that story. I can be assured a thousand times over that we all are important, significant, usable for good, but there's something about that story that helps me actually believe it in my heart. Imagery, either verbal or visual, is a powerful tool for communicating difficult-to-grasp spiritual truths and paradoxes. Imagery bypasses the skeptical mind and enlivens the spirit with a divinely irrational hope that transcends our earthly circumstances.

The Scriptures are full of examples of stories and imagery used to convey mysterious, salvific truths. Take the multiplication of the five loaves and two fishes, for instance. Christ invites us through this story to give Him our meager and imperfect little offerings of love, trusting that He can miraculously transform them into an abundance of nourishment for many. His Parable of the Good Samaritan powerfully illustrates what selflessly loving our neighbor looks like and requires of us.

Stories stick with me. I am thankful the Church understands this and has blessed us with a plentiful variety of amazing stories about our saints. Take St. Ia, for example. Her story is as whimsical and enthralling as a fairytale. Her anticipation, then disappointment, then wonder—they are all so relatable! I can picture her lying in bed, all restless and terrified, yet she is burning with excitement—the kind of anxious excitement I imagine Frodo Baggins must have felt before embarking on his journey from the familiar shire into the great unknown. For weeks, even months, more likely, she must have been prayerfully preparing herself—mentally, emotionally, physically, spiritually—for that morning she was finally to leave home in order to fulfill her destiny.

She must have slept fitfully, perhaps with one hand resting on the packed bag containing the few personal possessions she would bring with her. After a frustrating amount of tossing and turning, I imagine her eventually drifting off, only to bolt up with a start an hour later just as the sun was beginning to rise. This was the day! Like the Theotokos, she had said "yes" to emptying herself and bravely accepting God's calling to fulfill His will through her. So then imagine, just imagine how utterly devastated and disoriented she must have felt after sprinting breathlessly toward the shore, only to see her opportunity literally sailing away from her. What did it mean? Why, oh why, would God let this happen?

Oh friends, I have been there! I have been on that shore helplessly watching my best-laid plans abandon me, my head spinning with bewilderment and despair. I have felt the crushing blow of self-doubt and disillusionment in those awful moments of silence between the destruction of the life I assumed I'd have and the birth of a new reality fraught with loss and grace. There is so much I can identify with in the story of St. Ia and her seeming abandonment, and much I can learn from it. For this reflection, I will share with you two such lessons that have embedded themselves in my heart.

GOD BELIEVES IN ME EVEN if no one else does, including myself.

Now that I'm in my mid-forties, I've finally (for the most part) grown to accept and own my unique strengths and weaknesses, my distinct personality, and my Midwestern temperament. I have a dry sense of humor, zero sense of direction, and a tendency toward flightiness and wrestling with my faith. But for years, decades even, I would compare myself to others and try to emulate people I knew who seemed more pious than I was—or just seemed to have it more together in general.

As a new mother, these efforts involved a variety of homemade chore charts and sleep schedules suggested by whichever parenting book was trending at the moment, as well as a lot of sourdough starter after being in a moms' group where everyone made her own bread (and ground her own wheat). As a new Orthodox Christian, striving meant long rules of prayer and wordy, confident defenses of our decision to leave one Christian tradition and embrace another. I tried the "fake it till I make it" approach to looking, sounding, and acting like the perfect (fill in the blank), only to agonize in private over my inconsistencies and hypocrisy.

Eventually, after life had dealt us some difficult blows, and I had fallen flat on my face enough times, and my little children had grown into adolescents with their own minds, ideas, and wills, and after the Internet created a peace-smothering climate of divisiveness and cynicism, I sort of gave up on myself for a while. I was hanging onto faith by a thread. On the downside, I cried all the time and felt, like St. Ia, that I had been abandoned and left behind by God Himself and by others who were more stable and spiritually stronger than I was. On the plus side, I had been humbled.

In the story of St. Ia, the heart-wrenching death of her earthly expectations had to precede the infinitely more amazing and sustaining assurance of her preciousness to God. Having felt His compassionate and omnipotent presence in the miracle of the floating leaf, St. Ia journeyed forward with new courage, hope, and joy, knowing that God, who knew her more intimately than she even knew herself, had chosen her "as is" for that specific role and vocation.

At my lowest point, I clung to this account about a careless monk told by St. Nikolai Velomirovich:

*This monk was lazy, careless, and lacking in his prayer life; but throughout all his life he did not judge anyone. When dying, he was happy. When the brethren asked him how it was that with so many sins he could die joyfully, he replied: "I now see angels who are showing me a page containing my numerous sins. I said to them, 'Our Lord said: Judge not, and ye shall not be judged (Luke 6:37). I have never judged anyone, and I hope in the mercy of God that He will not judge me.' And the angels tore up the paper." Upon hearing this the monks were astonished and learned from it.*

"Don't judge anyone for anything" became my guiding principle, my mantra for hopefully finding some kind of redemption in the midst of my brokenness. If I couldn't will myself into a state of self-assurance and unwavering belief, then I would focus all my efforts on owning my identity as the for-real and true "chief among sinners." Mother Teresa wrote, "May God break my heart so completely that the whole world falls in," and that is exactly what suffering had mercifully done for me.

I have found that the more I seek to build bridges, find connections, and draw out beauty instead of zeroing in on what is ugly and hateful, the more courage, hope, and joy I experience. I journey forward into the great unknown, knowing that God, who knows me more intimately than I even know myself, has chosen me "as is" for this specific role and vocation as a flighty, Google-Maps-dependent, quick-to-laugh and slow-to-judge healing presence for others.

Heaven is here and now.

So there she is, standing heartbroken and forlorn on the shore, her vision blurred by tears and her throat scratchy from yelling. I like to imagine that everything has gone still, the birds have quieted their chirping, the bees have ceased buzzing, and even the wind has become tranquil and motionless. Before her, the water is transformed from turbulent waves to a sea of placidity. Without blinking, St. Ia fixes her gaze on a sole tiny leaf, floating peacefully, in no particular hurry, straight toward her. It is hypnotizing, this little leaf. And then, as if it were the most natural thing in the world, that leaf begins . . . growing! Through stillness and attentiveness, St. Ia is able to suspend disbelief and open her mind and heart to the miracle evolving right then and there in the present moment.

When my oldest daughter read the story of St. Ia, I asked her what stood out most to her about it. "I think it's cool how God uses ordinary things, like that leaf, to perform His miracles," she replied. I found that to be a lovely and thought-provoking observation. God chose a simple, humble leaf to be a conduit for His power and His glory. We find examples of this in Scripture as well, such as when God used mud to heal the blind man, those few loaves and fishes to feed the multitude, and a burning bush to speak to Moses. In the Holy Friday Matins service, we honor the wood on which Christ was crucified, singing, *The wise thief didst Thou make worthy of Paradise in a single moment, O Lord. By the wood of Thy Cross, illumine me as well and save me.*

I find it very compelling that Orthodox Christianity views the separation between earth and heaven not as a thick, impenetrable wall but rather as a veil so thin and transparent that the Kingdom of heaven is forever spilling onto us. The earth is bursting with heaven, but it takes stillness, attentiveness, and at least a mustard-seed–sized faith to recognize it in the ordinary people, encounters, and objects that surround us daily.

Last summer, my husband, Troy, and I made an effort to watch the sun set at the Indiana Dunes right by our house at least once a week. We'd drive there after dinner, walk to the shore, find a log to sit on, and then we'd stare in awe, usually in silence, as the sky exploded with color. It never got old. In fact, the more we made a habit of being observers of nature, the more spectacular not only sunsets but the changing leaves in autumn, the intricately woven bird's nest on our porch, the blooming daisies in our yard all became to me.

Perhaps the greatest tragedy of our current generation has been the diminishing of our attentiveness. Smartphones have made us addicted consumers of mind-titillating content who have forgotten the art of being. For those of us eternally minded, this is especially troublesome, as God is continuously revealing Himself with all His light, mercy, and hope in the small, ordinary details of our days.

When we anticipate finding snippets of heaven everywhere and anywhere, enlightening and encouraging us, then all our interruptions, conversations, and periods of waiting and observing take on brand-new significance; they become pregnant with possibility. There is no wasted time; all time is teeming with opportunities to pray, show kindness, learn patience, and create beauty. Even in—no, especially in—times of heartbreak and frustration, doubt and disappointment, it is imperative that we, like St. Ia, suspend disbelief and anticipate the miracle revealing itself. Our God is a God of love and resurrection! Seek Him and you will find Him. Knock, and He will answer. Trust that His ways are bigger than our ways. Come and see!

PERSONAL SURVEY

# A Resurrection of Hope

*For perfect hope is achieved on the brink of despair, when instead of falling over the edge, we find ourselves walking on air.*
—Thomas Merton

Have you ever felt discouraged from pursuing your heart's longing because of others' skepticism, or from boldly investing in the unique gifts God gave you because of your own self-doubt?

Sometimes God allows us to experience great anguish via loss before revealing to us His plan for our resurrection. Have you ever endured a season of loss or disappointment? How does St. Ia's story affect your perspective on those unanticipated trials and sufferings?

Can you remember an instance in the past when a closed door, though heartbreaking at the time, actually turned out to be an unexpected blessing?

_____
_____
_____
_____

Can you think of a time when God has intervened in your life in a miraculous and surprising way? What impact did that have on your faith?

_____
_____
_____
_____

What whispered invitations to participate in something divine have you discovered in moments of stillness?

_____
_____
_____
_____

OBSERVATIONS FROM A FRIEND

# *A Leap of Faith*

What unique gifts and talents do you admire in your friend? How have her gifts encouraged or inspired you?

_____
_____
_____

How has your friend been a cheerleader for you? How has she emboldened you to grow and evolve? Brainstorm with your partner ways to pay forward that optimism and support within your home, parish, and community.

_____
_____
_____

Share with your friend an example from your own life of a disappointment that later turned out to be a merciful blessing.

_____
_____
_____
_____

Make a list with your partner of big and small ways you can each say "yes" to God throughout your day. Be creative! Be specific!

_____
_____
_____
_____
_____

## JOURNAL PROMPT

# A Gift of Stillness

*God is everywhere. There is no place God is not. . . . You cry out to Him, "Where art Thou, my God?" And He answers, "I am present, my child! I am always beside you." Both inside and outside, above and below, wherever you turn, everything shouts, "God!" In Him we live and move. We breathe God, we eat God, we clothe ourselves with God. Everything praises and blesses God. All of creation shouts His praise. Everything animate and inanimate speaks wondrously and glorifies the Creator. Let every breath praise the Lord!*
—Joseph the Hesychast, 78th Letter

Tomorrow morning, wake up earlier than usual, pour yourself some coffee, and sit out on your front porch. Or if it's too chilly, just snuggle up on the couch with a blanket and look out the window.

For the first few minutes, clear your mind of thoughts and worries until you are quiet enough to hear the rhythm of your own steady breathing.

Now listen. Listen for God with loving anticipation, and look for Him in the trees, the birds, the rising sun. Allow yourself to be filled with the awareness of His presence.

From this state of prayerful stillness, now bring again to mind those nagging doubts, disappointments, and fears preventing you from finding peace and hope in the present moment. Write them down and imagine as you write them that you are removing them from your shoulders and laying them at the feet of Christ.

Now leave them there.

With your burdens lightened and your soul and mind abiding

in the here and now, begin to dig deep and write down a list of things you are grateful for, challenging yourself to find something salvific even in your difficulties and unanswered questions, like compassion born of humility and struggle.

Participate in the divine through attentiveness to the beauty in the ordinary blessings all around you. Wait expectantly for God to guide you, enlighten you, and sustain you through the ups and downs of the rest of your day, one moment at a time.

*Leaf ❧ Ia*

# DREAM

*Anna Neill*

# *You Are Nino*

You are Nino, and you are caught up in a noisy crowd on the streets of Mtskheta, in the country of Georgia. The clear sky glares down at the mass of people around you. You concentrate on keeping your feet on the ground and your head up, to avoid stumbling and being trampled.

You are new to this city, but you belong here as much as you belong anywhere. You have survived hundreds of miles of wilderness, persecution, wild animals, hunger, weather, and moments of despair between Jerusalem and this pagan city. You are alone in the world, except for the knowledge that you have dreamed a dream of the Most Holy Theotokos, and she has sent you out into this loneliness with her blessing. You carry a small cross, folded into being by her hands out of a grapevine, bound securely with your hair. Like your presence here, it is a thing you made together.

The road grows steeper. Ahead of you in the crowd, you see the king and queen of this place and the swirls of eager courtiers and subjects striving for their attention. This crowd is journeying to a mountain across the river from Mtskheta to worship a pagan idol, but there is nothing worshipful about them. Their talk is loud and worldly, their dusty bodies press thoughtlessly together, and you struggle always not to fall under their feet.

For several seconds, your memory conjures the day you walked to church to tell your Uncle Juvenal about the grapevine cross. You feel a fierce, silent peace, at odds with the pitiless horde around you.

The way is not so steep now; the noise increases sharply and then dies away into a panting silence. You have arrived.

Three idols stand at the mountain altar, and your stomach heaves as you compare them to the three figures on Mount Tabor. Today is the Feast of Transfiguration, and you wish with all your heart that the three before you were Jesus, Moses, and Elijah.

The worst of the idols is like a man, but not like a man. His giant body is clothed in golden chain mail. He wears a golden helmet, and his eyes are jewels—one a ruby, one an emerald, huge and glittering. "Armazi," the people murmur. Smaller gods attend him, a golden idol named Katsi on his right and a silver idol, Gaim, on his left.

Under the heated gaze of so many people, the idols seem vacant and grotesque. Turning your head, you see the faces on every side of you contorted with what passes for reverence. Your stomach heaves again as you catch words and sounds from the front of the crowd, where sacrifices are being prepared for the altar.

A trumpet blast startles you. Cymbals crash together, and you cover your ears involuntarily. You smell incense, but something is wrong with it. There is no sweetness in the scent.

The crowd around you plunges to the earth like stalks of wheat buckling under the blade of a scythe. Even the king and queen fling themselves down, and suddenly you are the only one standing in a sea of prostrate bodies.

Your heart burns. Who appeared on the mountain with your transfigured Lord? Moses and Elijah, a leader and a prophet! Why are you here, still standing in a crowd that has fallen down?

Because you are the only one, the only one of all these people who knows what they are missing.

Peter, James, and John threw themselves down on their faces, too, washed in the brilliance of uncreated light. None of the scores of people groveling around you knows anything about that. Not one of them.

But you do.

You close your eyes tightly, beating the sign of the cross into your head and breast with your clasped hands as a fervent prayer pours into your heart and tears wash the dust from your face.

"Almighty God!" Your voice stretches your tight throat. "By Your great mercy, bring this people to a knowledge of Yourself, the One, True God."

You draw breath, gulping down panic. Around you, a few shocked faces are turning up from the earth to stare at you.

"Scatter these idols as the wind blows dust and ashes from the face of the earth. Look down with mercy upon this people, whom You have created with Your almighty hand and whom You have honored with Your divine image!"

The prayer is holding you now. The seething crowd fades to a dim, humming sound at the outskirts of your consciousness.

"And You, O Lord and Master, did so love Your creation that You did give even Your only begotten Son for the salvation of fallen humankind."

Your gaze turns to the idols. You close your eyes and clench your diaphragm, pushing sound into your voice.

"Deliver the souls also of these Your people from the destructive power of the prince of darkness, who has blinded the eyes of their understanding so that they do not see the true path to salvation."

You have not been attacked yet, but the prayer is not finished.

"O Lord, grant me to see the final destruction of the idols standing here so proudly. So act that this nation and all the ends of the earth might comprehend the salvation given by You, that the north and the south together might rejoice in you, and that all nations might worship You, the one eternal God, and Your only begotten Son, our Lord Jesus Christ, to whom belongs glory forever."

You feel the air gathering itself around you. It makes a sound like an enormous, in-drawn breath. Your eyes open on rapidly fading light. Mountainous black clouds rear up like horses in the west and gallop through the sky above the river.

In an instant, everything has changed. The final words of your prayer are still breathing over your lips, and already men and women are scrambling to their feet. The king is shouting at his retinue. The queen is gesturing at the racing clouds, biting her fingers and weeping.

You remember Moses and Elijah on the mountain with Christ, and you do not run with the crowd. You know that any second now a stampede will begin, but you are already standing. You have that extra second in your favor.

You run away from the idols, to the rugged ground above them on the mountainside. God hid Moses in a cleft in the rock to save his life when He passed by. With your eyes on the rolling clouds, you seek out a cleft in the rock face and slip inside.

Down comes the rain like swords and arrows, bright as lightning, loud as thunder, shaking the earth and the air with its torrential power. The three idols topple onto the earth, prostrate as their fleeing worshippers had been. The raindrops shatter and crush them. Shards of gold and silver bounce into the air and drop into the formless heap. The temple behind them caves in on itself. The altar splinters as if an axe were laid to its root. The

*Dream ☉ Nino*

water gathers itself into currents, and the bones of the idols roar away down the mountainside, as meaningless as the other debris they will join in the swollen river below.

Nothing remains but the wet, clean earth and the blue sky revealing itself again as the storm passes.

You step out of your cleft in the rock, shaken with joy and wonder. At the sound of your prayer, the mountain was transfigured. It is only a small transfiguration. No one here can see God yet. But a place has been made empty, in preparation for His coming.

ON THE LIFE OF THE SAINT

# Nino

NINO WAS BORN into an illustrious Greek Christian family around 280 in Cappadocia. Her father, Zabulon, was a Roman army captain, a friend—or some accounts say, the relative—of St. George the Dragon Slayer. Her mother, Sosana, was the sister to Patriarch Juvenal of Jerusalem. Nino was their only, beloved daughter. In the raging persecutions during Emperor Diocletian's brutal reign, the holy parents moved to Jerusalem to be near the patriarch. They worked diligently to raise Nino in ascetic discipline from a young age. Their hearts were not in the world but longed for Paradise.

When Nino reached twelve years of age, her father received an ecclesiastical divorce from Sosana and was tonsured a monk. He went to labor for his salvation in the desert along the Jordan River, never to see his child again. The Patriarch Juvenal ordained his sister a deaconess, to serve in Jerusalem. Sosana gave her daughter to an older Christian woman, Sara, to finish raising her in the Faith and prepare her for adulthood. Nino was now bereft of her parents at a tender age, not from a fleshly death, but from the hunger for eternal life.

Sara had traveled in the Roman Empire as a young woman and, like Nino's parents, came to Jerusalem for a peaceful haven. Sara patiently taught her young charge all that she could of Christian doctrine. Nino gained wisdom beyond her years. The girl memorized the Gospels, reading them daily. When she read of Christ's seamless robe, she wondered where it had gone. Sara shared stories of the faraway land of Iberia, mountainous and full of strange pagan customs, where the Roman soldier had taken the robe after the Crucifixion. Rumors had said the robe remained in the city of Mtskheta. How could pagans hold such a dear relic with no faith in it?

There was another story Sara had told to Nino, one that was to change the course of her life. When the apostles had drawn lots for regions across the empire in order to spread the gospel after Pentecost, the Theotokos drew Iberia. As she was preparing to leave, an angel appeared to her, telling her to stay in Jerusalem as an anchor for the Church in a tumultuous time. It was said that she was bitterly disappointed but accepted the command and prayed for the mission she was never to achieve.

Nino ardently interceded with the Theotokos, asking her for the opportunity to visit Iberia in order to find the robe of Christ and continue the mission where the Holy Mother could not go. The young woman was rewarded. One night the Theotokos appeared to Nino in a vision, saying, "Go to Iberia and tell there the good tidings of the gospel of Jesus Christ, and you will find favor before the Lord; and I will be for you a shield against all visible and invisible enemies. By the strength of this cross, you will erect in that land the saving banner of faith in my beloved Son and Lord." When Nino awoke, in her hands was a cross made of twisted grapevines, tied with hair strands! To this day, the "drooping cross," with bent crossbar, is the national symbol for the Georgian Orthodox Church.

She immediately found her uncle, Patriarch Juvenal, showed him the grapevine cross, related the vision, and asked for his blessing to leave for Iberia. The patriarch saw the call as undeniable. He gave his blessing and arranged for Nino to travel with a contingent of fifty virgins who were fleeing persecution from Emperor Diocletian. Among the group was the princess Ripsimia, whom the emperor wanted to marry, though she had taken a vow of chastity for Christ's sake. When the party arrived in Armenia, King Tiridat saw Ripsimia and also wanted her as a wife. She refused again but could not escape the vengeance of the king. The princess and her companions were martyred, leaving Nino as the sole survivor.

Alone in a strange land, far from home and from her destination, Nino cried out to God for help. An angel appeared to her, telling her that when the roses were in bloom, she would see her consolation. Nino journeyed slowly for several months, learning the language and customs. She heard shepherds saying that the river before them flowed towards Mtskheta, where their pagan god was worshipped. Nino was afraid. How could she stand for the one true God and tell these people to abandon their former ways? Another dream came to her, in which Christ gave her a scroll with evangelical verses, including, "For I will give you a mouth and wisdom, which all your adversaries shall not be able to gainsay nor resist" (Luke 21:15).

Armed with her cross and now a scroll, Nino followed a caravan of pilgrims to Mtskheta to see the spectacle. There, joining the entourage of King Mirian and Queen Nana, Nino saw the gold and silver idols, placed high above the people. Her zeal burst out in exclamation as the pagan priests offered sacrifices. The weather opened in a terrible storm, the people fled, and Nino, like Moses, was tucked away in a rocky cleft to watch the hand of the Lord. The idols were washed away from the mountainside. For several days, the people searched for them but could not find them. In their fear, they began to doubt the power of their former gods and wondered which god could be great enough to sweep them away.

*Dream ○ Nino*

Nino returned to the city, this time anonymously, where she found lodging with the royal gardener and his wife, Anastasia. The strange young woman built a hut near the brambles and sang hymns to a god they could not see. Eventually, the couple was won over to the Christian faith, and to seal their conversion with a miracle, Christ granted them children, although they had previously been barren. The roses bloomed in the royal garden over Nino's hut.

Emboldened by joy, Nino began visiting with other families in the town. Her desire to find Christ's robe had not waned. She knew intuitively the relic would be key to helping her mission. She began visiting the Jewish quarter of town and asked polite questions about the robe, if any of the diaspora knew the legend. A story came together about a family who suddenly died because of the robe, and the last, a young girl, was buried with it by a cedar tree. Nino prayed at the location, having faith the Lord would grant miracles if the relic was nearby.

Nino redoubled her evangelistic efforts, and before long, King Mirian softened toward the gospel. He knew the Armenians were converting and recognized the turning tide. Without his idols, the king lacked a powerful anchor with his people. He did not hinder Nino's work, but he did not convert. His wife, Queen Nana, however, was malicious toward Christians and wanted to keep the pagan religions alive. She became ill and was near death. Her servants entreated the queen to send for Nino. In return, Nino wisely told the queen to visit her hut in the garden, knowing that an act of humility was a sign of faith. Queen Nana obeyed, and after the saint prayed for her, she was healed and confessed Christ.

King Mirian had one last hurdle to cross before repenting. He became angry with Nino because of her success, her miracles, and her fame. He planned in his heart to kill all the Christians, even his wife. The king went out to hunt one day in the mountains. Even at midday, it became as dark as night. In terror, he cried out a prayer to the God of Nino, promising to build a church and erect a cross. The darkness fled immediately. King Mirian returned to the city in joy and contrition. He found Nino, told her of the miracle, and they wept together.

Nino lived another dozen years after the king's conversion, working, praying, and teaching tirelessly to guide the country toward the true Faith. Before her death, she asked to be buried at Bodbe, in the eastern region of the country. King Mirian built a church there, dedicated to St. George. Her cross survived the centuries and is enshrined in the Cathedral of Tblisi.

STEPPING FURTHER INTO THE STORY

# Daring to Dream with Saint Nino

"MOM WOULD BE proud of me." Anyone who has lost a beloved parent when she was still a child or a young adult has paused at significant turning points in life to consider that phrase. When my mother reposed, I was thirty-three years old and still grappling with major life decisions. What did I want to do for a career? What did I want to accomplish here in whatever time God gives me? I had left outside employment two years previously to be her caregiver and the family anchor. I had not thought past each week, full of medical appointments and dinners to cook, let alone to the life I would eventually have to resume. The world stretched out before me as a blank slate. I was handed the pencil to write the next line in my life story. It was terrifying.

Abandonment, even with the holiest intentions, is a hardship. Death, peaceful and merciful for the infirm or a glorious martyrdom for the young, punches a hole in the fabric of life for those who remain. The desolate landscape after a wildfire hardly looks as though life could spring up through the ashes. A final choice is made. The door is closed. There is no going back.

Nino faced that same terror, twice: first, when her father left for the monastic struggle, and second, when her mother sought service within the Church. She had to grapple at a tender age with questions of where she could go and what she could do. For a young woman in the fourth century, the answers were predefined. Marriage to a pious young man, perhaps. Follow her parents in service to the Church. Monastic retreat from the world. Surely, that was all she could expect, right?

But God gave Nino stories—grand stories of a faraway place, an unfulfilled mission, a relic lost in the wilderness of paganism. We are shaped by stories, by what has been done and what might be possible. Nino heard of the Theotokos being called to go on a mission journey, as were all the other apostles. A small leap of imagination made it entirely possible that Christ would want another woman to fulfill His commandments. The enormous personal leap of faith is saying, "Let this be unto me according to your word."

At my mother's funeral wake, a hospice nurse named Marion, who loved our family through the final months, grasped my hands and firmly commanded, "You have to live now, baby girl. Ain't no one going to do it for you! You have a bigger job to do!" I had been faithful to the hidden tasks. The curtain was pulled back, and a stage awaited me. I could no longer hide from the world.

The lives of the saints show us that while the gospel commandments are the standard for everyone, obedience to Christ looks different in each time and place. We remember the saints precisely because they are individuals whose stories are irreplaceable in the life of the Church. God creates us with a diversity of talents that no one else will possess. He also creates us with the capacity to grow into His callings. We all have a bigger job to do, as long as it is in response to Christ.

When I have a moment where I feel that my mother would be proud of me, the task or goal I've accomplished is never anything she specifically spelled out for me. Rather, I have stretched toward what made me grow into a stronger version of myself. Her dream was that I would accomplish my dreams, go further than she was able to in life. I had to figure out on my own what those dreams were and how to get there. I didn't have a detailed map with directions to a crystalline vision. My planner nature would have carved a flat, smooth path of comfort and familiarity toward a frankly boring life. In my wildest dreams of a few years ago, I could never have envisioned the life and work I have now. Past Anna would never have said yes to what Current Anna is doing if she had seen it wholesale. Yet, here I am, doing what I thought impossible: working in a technical career at a prestigious organization, writing, teaching, and being married to a man uniquely suited to me in our interests and goals in life. I merely tried to make the next best choice that brought me closer to God.

How do we know what the next best choice is? "How can I, a fragile woman, perform such a momentous task, and how can I believe that this vision is real?" Nino asked when the Theotokos appeared to her. Discernment is a group task. Nino didn't run off to the northern latitudes with her grapevine cross immediately, with the full gusto of a divine directive. She sought her Uncle Juvenal's advice and blessing. Other Christians serve as our collective mirror. We could be flat-out deceived through our pride or overly enthusiastic to start right now when we should wait.

Nino's journey took many months as she went slowly into a new landscape, people, and languages. She built relationships with familiar people from her former home in Jerusalem, the Jewish diaspora. She shows us we need to take time to learn, to prepare for our dream. The pivotal moment of crying out against idols would have been impossible if she had not known the words to use. When we see the moment, our voice and muscles will know what to do.

As the Theotokos appeared to Nino and handed her a fragile grapevine cross, telling her to go to the Iberian people, she imparted to Nino the motherly gift of bravery. Do what I could not, experience all I wanted to see and hear. You have the ability. You are enough. You are never alone. Keep going! It was no coincidence that the Theotokos and Nino had parallel lives in many respects: virgins, both given over to be raised for a holy purpose at a young age, who saw that God wanted their obedience for the growth of the Kingdom. The Theotokos, of all women, knew what Nino would face—ostracism, doubt, and hardship.

A few months after my mother's funeral, I was baptized into the Orthodox Christian Faith. I was still experiencing bouts of crushing grief, of missing her physical presence, her words of wisdom. At confession, my priest pointed to the icon of the Theotokos and said, "She is your mother now." It was like he joined our hands, and the Holy Mother led me toward the Church as my sanctuary and rock. I learned to ask her for guidance, for protection, for discernment. She built trust with me as I saw clearly how she answered my requests.

Nino had to go it alone as, again and again, she was stripped of physical companionship. God had one messenger for the Georgians, and it was a small Cappadocian girl. Like her, when you step out in obedience for a new task, you will be tempted to underestimate yourself, and others will discount you. We call that feeling "imposter syndrome": I shouldn't be here, with these people who are better than me, trying to achieve an impossible goal. Your voice will quaver. You will want to hide. You may even flounder at the first try. In that moment, trust that the invitation to participate in divine love is the affirmation that you are enough. "He might make known the riches of His glory on the vessels of mercy, which He had prepared beforehand" (Rom. 9:23). God is working through you and with you.

After my mother's death, I slowly began to make choices rooted in what I deeply loved from a young age. Reading, helping others, and curiosity all lent themselves to pursuing a degree in library science. I volunteered and then worked at a museum. Another major life upheaval after I had finished my degree launched me out from the home I had known for ten years and into a completely new city. There I connected with a mission parish that needed the talents of every adult member. Would I teach Sunday school to middle-school–aged girls? Nothing like taking on a responsibility you never had before! Teaching then grew into the dialectic of writing. Saying yes to fulfilling the needs before me opened up many more avenues to service than I had dared dream.

Mourn what you lose for the sake of Christ, but know that whatever you leave behind or whatever is taken from you, Christ will grant back to you, though sometimes in a different wrapper. "Do not seek all at once, but gently, and little by little, ascend this ladder that leads you up to Heaven" (St. John Chrysostom, Homily 63 on Matthew). Oh, the joy that Nino had with her first convert and sister in Christ, Anastasia! To go from being a solitary Christian to having fellowship is immediate life and breath.

I can attest that whatever I have lost for obedience to Christ has been added back to me in a myriad of better ways.

PERSONAL SURVEY

# *Dream the Hard Things*

Dreams are like seeing the mountaintop from the valley. What are visions you have for yourself that are only in the big picture right now? Are they fuzzy visions or sharp outlines?

_____
_____
_____
_____

When you look at your aspirations and gifts, where do you feel you are too weak to carry them out? What is the hinge point where you say, "That is impossible"?

_____
_____
_____
_____

Where have you felt underestimated by others? Where do you underestimate yourself? Does self-doubt make you shrink back from obedience? Does it fuel your ambition to prove others wrong?

_____
_____
_____
_____

Where do you need to speak the truth in your dream? How will that look?

What is one aspect of your life dreams that will further the dreams of others? How can you "own" it with your unique voice and talents?

Consider the poverty of your understanding and limited vision. What are you holding onto out of fear of loss?

OBSERVATIONS FROM A FRIEND

## Awakening Lost Dreams

*Hope deferred makes the heart sick,*
*But when the desire comes, it is a tree of life.*
—Proverbs 13:12

Everyone carries with her unfulfilled dreams. We think the door has closed or too much time has elapsed. Sit with your partner and draw out one to three dreams she has nurtured in her heart but has not spoken out to another person. There are no limits! Simply say, "This is what I would like to do and have not accomplished yet."

_____

_____

_____

Look for ways your friend can work toward those dreams. If she thinks age, infirmity, or any other current stage of life prevents her from pursuing them, think of ways the dreams could be shared with others who might catch the vision. Nino began her mission alone, but as the angel promised, she did not labor without help.

_____

_____

_____

_____

Do you both struggle with the question of where to begin? As St. John Chrysostom says, "Every work which does not have love as its beginning and root is nothing." Look for areas around you that lack love, care, service, and truth. Ask, "Lord, what would You have me do?" and you will find yourself busier than you thought possible!

When trials come, does your friend shrink back? Does she feel like she has to carry the burden of her work alone? Help her talk through the difficulties. Is her pride involved, where she thinks only she can do the work perfectly? How can you help? How can others help?

JOURNAL PROMPT

# Your Mission, Should You Choose to Accept It

*Do not be cast down over the struggle—the Lord loves a brave warrior. The Lord loves the soul that is valiant.*
—St. Silouan the Athonite

THE TIME OF complete desolation is when God plants the seeds. A cleared garden bed is a blanket of dirt, full of promise for what should grow in it. Vigilance keeps out the weeds, the cares of life that choke out the intended harvest. Look over your activities and obligations right now. If your life were a garden, which season are you in? Do you have an abundance of relationships and connections that are building toward a harvest of good things? What is choking out your intentions to live valiantly?

Have you experienced a "clearing," where obligations have been removed from you? After the flood of grief subsides, you will be able to view yourself as available to God in a way you were not before. Are you willing to open your heart for what God will give as consolation for what was lost?

*Dream* ☽ *Nino*

# RIVER

*Summer Kinard*

# *You Are Piama*

Y OU OPEN YOUR eyes to the sound of a water bird's wings. The bird is on the way to the river that flows wide and deep on the other side of the path that goes past your back garden. You can smell the water. The mist off the Nile has covered you like a blanket while you slept. The harsh sackcloth fibers of your garment are heavy and strong with the damp, and your hem dips to your ankles when you rise and stretch your arms out to your sides to pray.

You make the sign of the cross and bend through the cloud to touch the hard-packed earth, careful to be silent. You don't wish to wake your mother, who sleeps on a pallet across the room from your thin mat. You finish your prayer and pad on silent feet into the tree-lined garden behind the house.

You fix the large clay jars onto your water yoke and walk through the kitchen garden to the fig trees, dark and silent in the pre-dawn light, to listen. There are no footsteps this early. The cloud and the hour will hide you from the notice of the villagers. You make your way across the path and down to the river's edge. You listen for the trickle of water into the dugout hollow made by the washing women. The water there is cleanest to drink before they stir it up. The hollow will disappear under the silt when the autumn floods come, but the women will dig it out again in winter. You are grateful for their work for the common good. You will ask Mother to give the women some of the strong twine you spin to help them in their work.

You feel forward with your toes until they brush against the sandstone step. There. You descend, careful not to catch the water jars in the reeds that bow their heads toward the path. Five steps down into the clear water. You count them through your soles. In your soul, you count the five wounds of the Lord: His feet—one, two; His side; His hands—one, two. You are in the water. Your garment wraps around your calves, its rough strands a stark contrast to the smoothness of the water. You bow low to fill the jars, and you remember the bishop touching the cross to the water when he blessed it. All the waters of the world are blessed by Christ's Baptism. This water is blessed. The mist above the water hugs you close as you rise.

Your world is in this mist. Your vow has bound you to your house by the river and the fruit and nut hedge that surrounds your house and the church that is a short walk along the river path. Even when you go to church, the world is hidden from you by the morning mist.

You think of how the water swells the grains and rets the flax and ferments the wheat in the three clay jars where you store your daily bread. You were there, toes in the muddy shore, when the bishop, clothed in white cloth that you had woven, came to the water and blessed it. In Christ's Baptism, all waters of creation were blessed, and the waters from above and below mingled and spread life. Life comes each year after the floods that feed and wash the fields.

You return home with the heavy jars of water and set them down near the oven in the outdoor kitchen. You clink open a clay bread jar and scoop out the sour sprouted grain. The morning breeze carries the river scent to you, and there is trouble in the water. You see before you the clay oven and the dense dough that will become the chewy loaves for you, Mother, and the beggars. You flick a drop of water onto the hot clay baking surface. It sizzles and steams. But there. You catch on a memory and wait.

"O Lord," you pray. "What is it You show me?" A glimpse of memory: the people lift their faces to the blessed droplets of water falling over them. But one of the droplets is a tear. You see it amongst the myriad drops of the one water. It falls from the Cross of Christ, the one on Calvary and the one in the bishop's hand, both at once, and splashes into the mud between the villages. You look up quickly, almost catching sight of the Lord as He cried, almost feeling the holiness of the water seep through your headscarf and through your hair and into your heart to water the seeds of life. You remember that an angel of the Lord would touch the water to bring healing, and you draw a deep breath. Is the angel come now? You shut your eyes against the brightness that follows on the glimpse of the Lord.

"Piama, dear one, what has frightened you?" You turn toward the warm sound of your mother's voice. Her brow is furrowed with worry. "You saw trouble in the water again."

You nod and place the last loaf into the oven alongside the rest.

"I'll finish here," Mother says. She waits for you to clean the sourdough from your hands, then hands you your wooden drop spindle.

You take the spindle into the room with the icons and the flax. You sense that your prayer will be long today, so you take up long fibers for your spinning. You smile at the smooth strong thread you are spinning. Mother and you will weave the fine thread tight and bleach the cloth white in the sun. It will be a tithe to the Lord that will clothe the bishop and the orphans in his care.

The thwoo-thwoo-thwoop of the spindle sets the rhythm of your prayer. You say, "Holy, holy, holy." You drop and spin until the midday demon of acedia comes to distract you. You notice the numbness in your spinning hand and the pinching twist in your knee and hip. You notice the hunger in your belly and the dryness of your tongue. "Holy" is a whisper now nearly drowned out by the soft rhythm of the flax. You focus on the flaxen song and remember. Christ was wrapped in linen at His birth. "Holy, holy." He was stripped of linen at His Passion. "Holy, holy." He was wrapped in a linen shroud at His burial. "Holy, holy." He tore open the linen veil of the temple at His Resurrection. "Holy, holy, holy." You do not notice acedia any more. You notice the holiness of the love of Christ spinning through your hands in the linen gospel of memory.

Thwoo-thwoo-thwoop the spindle sings, and you hear it like the snapping of each strong thread in the temple veil. You say "Holy" to the song of the tearing. It is opening a vision of the love of Christ. It is tearing in your heart. You lean into the waiting. When will you see Him? "Come," your heart says, "seek His face. Your face, Lord, will I seek."

You are so consumed in the heat of the work and the quiet that you are surprised to feel the evening breeze. You let your eyes rest in gratitude upon the icons of the Crucifixion and the Mother of God embracing the infant Lord. Mother enters the room, passing between you and the icons with a reed to light the lamps that sit in front of them.

You pause your work and set aside the spindle and the flax. You go through the two rooms of the house to the backyard kitchen where you made the bread that morning. The loaves are wrapped in a rough linen cloth inside a basket. You pick it up and turn to go inside, but you stop when you see movement in the fig tree by the corner of the house.

You go to the tree and hold out your hand in front of the leaves. Two small children of three or four years take your hand. You lead them out of the shadows. They are ashen and thin with hunger. You hand bread to each of them. They stare at you in astonishment. A loaf of bread each, and not even kicks or begging to get it. They hug the bread to themselves cautiously, waiting to see if you mean it. You have smelled the bread, too, and your mouth waters enough to let you speak.

"Pray for Piama, dear ones of Christ." You make the sign of the cross over yourself and bow your head toward the children. They smile and push through your small garden to the path. Their village is a few miles away. They will reach home at nightfall, to share their bounty, no doubt, with other children and women grown quiet with hunger.

You take the last loaf inside for Mother. She has brought water mixed with a little wine to the table, along with greens and pistachios. You pray with her and gratefully eat the food she gives you. She speaks of trades she made that day and of the good work of the loom. She tells you that the thread today is good and strong. "It will do well for giving, but Piama, I want you to take a little of the cloth for yourself, too. You wear sackcloth the way other maidens wear finery."

You fold your hands and look down.

Mother relents. "At least I hope you will let me give you a fine veil."

You nod, surprised at the symmetry of the Lord's gifts. You have prayed all day for the veil to be parted, and Mother will cover you in a veil she weaves from the thread you spun with that prayer.

A realization rushes past you like a broken thread. You listen for the "Holy" in the falling night. "Mother," you say, looking up from the teardrop in the mud to the One on the Cross, "I must go to the river."

"There are night creatures there already. Stay. We have water enough for the evening."

You listen. You hear, "Holy, holy, holy," and it is being sung not only by your heart but by a great voice. "I hear singing. I will not be harmed."

Mother nods and follows you to the door. In the fading twilight, you cross the garden, then the road, and walk downhill to the river.

You pause before you come to the steps. The mud under your feet holds the day's heat, and you can scarcely tell where your feet end and the warm mud begins. "Clay from clay, I am only mortal, though God has breathed on me," you whisper. A great silence swallows your words and stills the night sounds of the river. "Holy" sings out in the falling mist before you, and the sound trembles through your head and chest and hands and toes, through the mud and the river and the linen, and you are seized with the white-hot terror of holiness. You are like clay when it is dipped in molten gold, and you feel your lips, even through the burning, move to answer, "holy."

"Do not be afraid, Piama," the voice says. You close your eyes against the light, and you see again the visions: the Lord crying on the Cross, the bishop blessing the waters and the people, the teardrop on the ground between the villages. You know the reputation of the village with the hungry children. The men are greedy and violent, prone to pillaging other villages. They burn houses and enslave their inhabitants. This is old news. The angel shows you this in a moment rather than telling you. Then you hear a shift in the song—"holy" sung as a dirge.

The angel has come to warn you. "The murderers are coming for your village."

You draw breath to ask that they be spared, but the angel is already departing, the mournful song ringing like bells over the water. "Holy, holy, holy," you weep. The night quiets. The water stills. Wind blows over the reeds, and you suddenly know what you must do. You run back to your home to your waiting mother.

"The village is going to be attacked in the morning. Our neighbors who neglect the starving slave children will come and seek to take our lands. They will kill us for the water, for they are jealous of our prosperity." The teardrop is a warning of broken community. "Mother, the elders must know."

You clean the cups and dishes while Mother goes to the elders. It is almost fully dark now, but you recognize their voices when they approach the house. You bring the pitcher of mixed wine and the pistachios, still untouched from your interrupted meal, and set them before the elders. You tell them, "The village that comes against us is stronger than us and will destroy us. Boastful and violent men have taken up staves and spears to kill us. You must go and meet them while they are far off, so that perhaps they will be turned back."

The old men and women are the color of fire in the lamplight as they listen. As one, they begin to implore you.

"Oh, Piama, blessed by God, go to the next village at once and tell them that their plan has been revealed by the Lord. This will strike fear into their hearts, and they will lay aside their evil intentions," they say. "We cannot fight off a band of desperate men. They outnumber us. We beg you on our knees, go to them."

You look from the wizened faces to the taut forehead of your mother's bowed head. Over her head you glimpse the icon of the Crucifixion shining from the corner of the back room. You remember the teardrop and the water and the holy.

"I will not leave my home," you say, and the words make you

brave as you speak them. "But you may leave this with me. May the glory of the Lord be revealed."

One by one, the elders come to you and kiss your face and make the sign of the cross over you. Mother sees them out, then she returns and stands before you.

"My Piama, take a little to drink so that your prayers will flow throughout the night. I will fill the lamp."

You go to the bedroom, but you do not roll out your sleeping mat. Tonight there will be no rest. You make the sign of the cross over yourself and kiss the Lord's feet in the icon. You begin to pray, but the mist is already swirling through the cracks in the door to cover the floor. You take the lamp to the garden to light your way to the ladder. You set the lamp in the stand on the wall by the ladder and climb up to the roof. As you climb, the mist falls beneath you. You are standing as above a cloud. Your whole life is hidden in that cloud, and you are hidden with Christ in God.

All day, you have called out "holy" to the pattern of your daily work. Now you are overwhelmed by that word, as the rains flood the Nile and nourish the entire region of Kemet. You feel your mouth form the word, but you cannot hear yourself any longer. You have entered into the great quiet of vision and of love.

"Holy" the hungry children in your fig trees. "Holy" the fathers whose crops dried up in the heat. "Holy" the desperate mothers trading their ailing geese instead of the eggs. "Holy" the enemies who have fallen into the pit of covetousness. "Holy" the desire for food and water that God placed in the hearts of men. "Holy" the God who feeds us from His own hands. You see the people for whom you pray as faces rising through the mist, kind and hostile, neighbor and stranger washed with the water, washed with the tear from Christ's eye.

Your arms, strong from the day's work, tremble as you lift them at your sides. You hold each person in the flood of love and call out the holiness in him or her until the mist stirs around your feet with the morning breeze. A strike of flax in the corner moves in the wind as well, and you know that God has done it. The violence of your neighbors has retted away.

As the final watch of the night thickens to the darkness before dawn, you sing out a prayer in a voice strengthened by the faith of all the Church, men and women, children, and angels. "O Lord, You Judge of the earth, who have no pleasure in whatever is iniquitous, O my Lord, when the prayer which Your handmaiden prays and her supplication reach You, let Your power transfix the enemy in the spot wherein they are."

You walk out through the back garden and onto the path by the fig trees. You walk until you are at the uttermost end of the village. You stop. You do not hear footsteps. The sun rises. The birds start up their song. The elders come and stand behind you on the path. The mist clears in swirls and gusts. There, a stone's throw before you, are the faces of the neighboring villagers, damp with dew and streaming tears. They are silent, frozen, until the mist rises and you see the elders step forward in the brightening day. You retreat to the confines of your garden just as the attackers begin to stir. They have set down their weapons and make signs of peace to the elders.

You step into the cool of the garden and hear the ones who were your enemies praising God in joyful voices. "Thanks be to God, who through the prayers of the maiden Piama has delivered us."

ON THE LIFE OF THE SAINT

# Piama

MOST OF THE time my laundry isn't interrupted by angelic visitations. Nonetheless, I have pinned on the wall beside my washing machine a holy icon of St. Piama and a scan from a 1907 translation of her life from *The Paradise of the Holy Fathers*.* In that volume, St. Piama has one closely set typed page devoted to her life, which ended in peace in AD 337. Chapter 35, "Of Piamon the Virgin," sets up her story by way of a sketch that might have fitted many dedicated virgins of her time: She lived all her days with her mother, kept vigil at night, ate once a day at evening, and worked at the weaving of linen. The story takes a sudden turn when we learn that Piama "was held worthy of the gift of knowing what was going to happen before it happened." This brief introduction of Piama's faithful life is followed by a vivid description of the violent history of murders over wealth and water in the Nile delta of Piama's time.

St. Piama lived somewhere outside of Alexandria, Egypt, in the delta region known as Kemet. Since we only know that Piama's village in the delta region was closer to water than their neighbors and that she spun and wove flax, I set Piama's story on a rise above the Nile, in a village that would have been in the middle of floods each autumn.

Every year when the rains came, the Nile would flood the fields of the river delta, enriching the soil with silt so that it produced

---

\* Translated out of the Syriac by Ernest A. Wallis Budge, M.A., Litt.D., D.Lit. (London: Chatto & Windus, 1907).

large crops of flax, wheat, barley, and other crops. These floods also fed into a series of canals that shunted water into vast, several-stories-high networks of cisterns under the ancient city of Alexandria, which was built in a desert coastal area that was too close to the sea to have fresh well water. Those fields and cisterns raised the stakes on the control of the water in the delta until, as *The Paradise of the Holy Fathers* tells us, "there came against the inhabitants of her village a crowd of boastful and violent men carrying staves and spears to kill them."

But the reason I like to think about St. Piama when I do the laundry is not to do with her context of intense struggle—let the reader understand!—but because of her life of prayer woven into the making of linen cloth. Flax cultivation was already a millennia-old tradition in Egypt by the time Piama lived. The flax grew in large fields. In the spring, the pale blue flax flowers would have brightened the land around Piama's home. The holy images of St. Piama sometimes show her headscarf of such a blue color, and I like to think of her delight in praying in those flowered fields, hidden by the color of heaven.

In the late summer, the flax would be harvested by pulling it up by the roots. It would be rippled to separate the seeds from the stalks, left to ret (rot) in water, broken to remove most of the outer parts of the plant, scutched (beaten with specially designed wooden tools) so that the long fibers separated from the outer structure of the plant, and hackled through large combs to stretch out the fibers and separate the longest, finest fibers from the shorter utilitarian ones. Once the fibers were prepared, there would follow long months of spinning, weaving linen cloth, bleaching the linen white in the sun, and sometimes dyeing the bleached cloth. The spinning and weaving of flax into linen cloth, we are told by Holy Tradition, was Piama's work. She most likely used a drop spindle, the most efficient method of her time, so I wrote that rhythm into her prayers and daily work.

The tradition of praying while working with one's hands was widespread in the Christian world by Piama's time. The monastic pioneers known as the Desert Fathers often wove ropes and baskets to accompany their prayers. But handiwork as a sacred practice goes back even further. In the Book of Exodus, God gives the spiritual gift of craftsmanship, pouring the Holy Spirit out upon people who designed and carved, wove and sewed and gilded for the creation of the Tabernacle of His Presence. In Exodus 31, we hear God say, "and I have given skill to all the skillful." If you have not read that chapter in a while, read it before you revisit the story of Piama. Look at how the Holy Spirit pours out gifts for craftsmanship. That gift that God gave for the making of the tabernacle still comes upon those who seek God with prayer as they work, and God doubtless made Piama's handiwork holy. Since Piama was a Christian, she and her mother probably dedicated some of the finest linen they produced to the use of the church.

Piama was also a dedicated virgin. Though we don't often hear the term "virgin" used as an honorific title these days, in Piama's time it was a sign of great respect for her faith. To call her Piama the Virgin was not only to acknowledge her unwedded state, but to praise the purity of heart that resulted from her dedicated prayers to God. During the early centuries of the Church, sexual renunciation through virginity was a common practice for those who wished to dedicate their lives more fully to prayer. Piama thus held a position of respect in her community even though she lived her life almost entirely within the walls of her garden and home. Being a homebody or an unmarried spinster did not warrant especial praise, but being a spinster homebody for Christ's sake and in order to engage in unceasing prayer was a worthy calling, respected by pagans and Christians alike.

Piama's prayers would likely have centered on Psalms, spiritual songs, passages of Scripture, and prayers of the heart, most likely drawn from Scripture. Prayers of the heart are usually small words or phrases repeated in the course of a breath or the rhythms of daily work. Today, many people pray the Jesus Prayer in this manner: "Lord Jesus Christ, Son of God, have mercy on me, a sinner." Yet when I read the story of Piama, I was struck by the casual way the historian tells us that "the angel of the Lord appeared unto her." I chose to give her an older prayer and one that evoked the song of the angels, such as the one who visited her. "Holy, holy, holy!" sang the seraphim in Isaiah's vision in the temple (Isaiah 6), and in Jewish and Christian services around the world ever since, the faithful pick up that refrain and sing it as their own heart's song.

STEPPING FURTHER INTO THE STORY

# Settling Down with God

I LIVE ON the starling path. Every sunset in winter, thousands of starlings form a murmuration over our heads as my family and I watch with glee. My children call the birds a force field, and they are right. The birds pour through the sky in a fifteen-minute swath of song and delight. I feel the joy of them like the joy my mother Eve must have felt in the first garden under the first sky, when the starlings prepared the way of the Lord to walk with her and Adam in the cool of the evening. Piama had her mist, and I have my starlings.

Like Piama, I make my home in the bend of a river. Like her, I pray while I move my hands. Because we're all autistic in my family, I also love being at home as Piama did. It's safer here, kinder, and every room is arranged to help us settle down with God. Settling down is on my mind, because as I write this we moved house only a few months ago.

Moving house creates upheaval that invites us to sort our luggage from our baggage. I write this in a half-unpacked office, surrounded by sacred books and images, my favorite sheets of hand-printed art papers, a stack of balloons ready to be inflated in the six-week spree when more than half my family has birthdays, and a second desk filled with occupational therapy aids for me to help my children grow through their disabilities. We always grow around some center idea of ourselves, and I want the children's centers to be shaped like the presence of God. But how can I teach them to find something we believe without seeing? For that, I look to Piama.

Piama's great gift of steadiness in prayer was not that she once saw an angel and saved her village with an intercessory prayer. Her great gift was that she recognized the word of God when He spoke to her. She filled her contained life with habits of prayer until every part of her daily pattern was a live circuit connecting her with God.

Oh, how I wish my life were like that! But moving house has made me aware of the paucity of grace that I set before my eyes sometimes. Because I am relatively isolated by my family's extreme needs, I use the internet to connect with friends and to communicate with the wider world. Oftentimes, I thank God for the people and churches and joys and testimonies of God's love that I see there. But there is a lot about life online that is not graceful. There are disputes, controversies, a barrage of tragedies and travesties and the brokenness of people who have collapsed in on themselves instead of breaking to let the light in. When I see these stories, I am tempted to seek power instead of permanence, to win an argument instead of a heart.

That's when Piama speaks to me, steady as the river. I walk with her into the hiddenness of mist and prayer. These three endure: faith, hope, and love, and the greatest of these is love. I stand in the prayer corner in the quiet after some night noise has awakened me. In the coolness of the night, there is no heat left to controversies, no hot air to raise my opinions above others'. I ask for mercy for my shortcomings, and I wait. Like a wind I hear a truth, and my memory sees Piama standing there on her roof, hands raised, and bowing low, beseeching. Faith is the great gift, and it has been handed down to me by my mothers like a strong garment that does not wear out, woven with the whispered words of prayer.

Seek what endures. Build faith. Your prayers are more powerful than a thousand political weapons. And there, at the end, as I let my memory wrap around the story to show me my foremother Piama, so alone in her life of seclusion, I see another gift, this one of self-revelation: All of your temptations come from fear of being alone.

A few days later, I call my spiritual father to ask him what this means. He listens to me patiently as I ramble through visions and prayers and practical matters and parties. Then he tells me what I need to hear. I have learned how to dispense with baggage, the emotional weights I no longer need after healing from past traumas, but some of what I have brought with me to this new place is luggage filled with good gifts to set up our home. "Settle down with God," he tells me, and I laugh, thinking of how long I have stared this truth in the face without seeing it.

For months, as we have unpacked and set up house, I have read Piama's story and prayed alongside a holy image of her in prayer. I have thought about how she shaped her solitude around faith, but I had not seen the obvious. She was not alone. With all her dedication to reclusiveness, she shows me how to settle down with God.

Praying while I work, holding fast to that which endures, and seeking God when conflicts arise: these are how I settle down with God. They're the same for me in my house filled with children under the starling path as they were for Piama, spinning the strong cloth of prayer in the mist of solitude.

Like Piama, I am an ordinary mystic. I pray with busy hands and love to hide away. Like her, I do not find power in confrontation and argument, but in faith that has rooted itself throughout my life and my home. Often in my daily routine, I feel a nudge and hear a still, small voice whispering over the frying onions or the susurrus of folding clothes and turning pages. Faith is the treasure.

When I listen, when I heed the instinct to inquire of the Lord for the wisdom He gives so freely, I find myself knowing what to do to help my nonverbal son speak, or to pull my sensory-overwhelmed daughter back from the brink of meltdown. I cannot lose a faith that has grown up all around me, because I know where to find it. The path of holiness is laid at my feet, and that path is made of dirty laundry and spilled rice. It is the way of the Lord, prepared for me to meet Him. I prepare the way for Him to dwell with us when I receive with gratitude the gift of a life at home.

Don't get me wrong. My home is not a showpiece. It's a home-in-progress, both because we're still unpacking and because we are in progress. There are pictures stacked in corners waiting to be hung on empty walls, and inexplicable pieces of tape that find their way into my shoes and blankets. I have a household filled with extroverted thinkers with communication challenges, which looks like this: art supplies and prayer books and candles and games and play sand and blocks and sensory toys flowing and ebbing over tables between meals. I thank God that we have these tools and this space to build each other up, even though it means we have the added work of tending to the tools and space.

I didn't always value my home-in-progress. The chief gift of shelter isn't its perfection or how well it's organized. Homes endure because they are a place for faith to grow. My mind and body form around the places I frequent. My memories layer over walls, over habits, over the prayer corners and decorations of my home. At home, I learn that God knows where to find me. And this is the best part! I learn that I am not alone after all. Home is where I settle down with God. God waits for me in every room, and I learn there to wait for Him, too.

I was taught—falsely—that prayer is a separate type of work, a separate work, or separate from work: that in order to count, it has to be compartmentalized and set apart from our daily life. But this is a lie. I am to follow Piama's example and to pray without ceasing, making my *Kyrie eleisons* with laundry in my hands and saying "Our Father" while I hand a cup of water to a child. Yet, even in the steadiest habits of prayer, sometimes crises come.

In my own life, I remember the panic I felt the first time my youngest son was diagnosed with severe autism. Questions and uncertainties rushed up at me from a piece of paper telling me that my son had almost no discernible communication or cognitive abilities. But I am not a panicker. I am a believer. I have believed when I couldn't see for my whole life. I went to my prayer corner and looked at the cross and begged the saints to pray for us and told God I needed Him. "You taught St. Anthony to read by sending him angels," I said, pointing my finger right at the Lord's face as I said it. "I don't know what I'm doing." I glanced at my son and pointed from the cross to the small boy at my knee. "You teach him to read." I didn't stop to wonder if two-year-olds without language could learn to communicate, and I didn't expect that faith would remove all hardship from the path. All I needed was a divine foundation so I could know where to stand and go forward.

When my son spelled his first word in letter magnets a couple of days later—*Hodegetria*, the Greek word for the Mother of God that means "She who shows the way" to her Son—I thought it was probably not a coincidence. But I wasn't totally sure, so I went to the prayer corner again and asked God to keep it up. The next week, we watched as our twenty-six-month-old son spelled on the magnet board "Go Down Stairs" when he wanted to go down to play in our backyard. God heard my prayer and taught my son to read.

Not every moment of faith ends in a desired outcome. Most of Piama's prayers are hidden from us in the mist of God's covering love. Most of my prayers fly off like birds, and I do not even remember them once they're prayed. But it happened that I read that diagnosis in the doorway right next to the place in my kitchen where I went to pray. There was no mighty wind or lightning or mist when I turned my body toward the cross, but it was that moment when the first miracle happened: I knew that God was there to help us.

God is here to help us. When I see this truth, I settle down with God. For Piama, settling down with God looked like feeding her faith with a virginal life of prayer and working flax into cloth while hidden in her mother's house. Piama wasn't surprised when God sent her a word. She had been waiting on it her whole life.

For me, settling down with God means feeding my faith with prayer, hospitality, communication, song, and discussions in the midst of family life. Faith, hope, and love endure longer than strong cloth and strong tea and arms strengthened by the burdens of prayer and making a home where God is expected. She wove, and I write. We both set about our work with faith, expecting God to show up.

I rise in the night and feel my faith drop into place like a heavy garment. It is not only my faith that shields me, but also the faith of all my fathers and mothers before me, and the faith of Christ Himself. The shield of faith endures and is a strength given by God, who is my strength. The Psalms ring out from my heart and my lips, over shadowed corners, over laundry, the dishes, the soup pots, the children, the papers on my desk. I sing, and like the starlings on their force-field road and the mist of prayer that hid Piama, I set between my household and the world the power and the love of God. "Holy God, Holy Mighty, Holy Immortal, have mercy on us."

PERSONAL SURVEY

# *Expecting God*

Were you surprised to learn that God blesses creative activities? Are there things that you make? In what ways can you offer the creative process in prayer?

_____
_____
_____
_____

Do you have repetitive patterns in your daily work that would fit with the rhythm of prayer the way Piama was able to pray while she worked? Think about your morning routine. Is prayer part of the work you do when you get up? What about your midday stretch? Evening routines? Have you tried praying a short prayer over and over while you knit or crochet?

_____
_____
_____

How does the church year with its seasons help you measure time and weave prayer and time together? Is there any part of your work that you feel is detached from prayer?

_____
_____
_____

One of the ways to begin to pray is to ask God to help you begin. Write down the places and patterns in your life where you want to begin with God.

In mystery novels and shows, detectives look in the kitchen to see whether someone lives alone or with family, and whether he or she had or expected company. Look at your table and kitchen. Does anything around those spaces remind you to expect God?

Do you have spaces set aside in your home dedicated to prayer? Rooms tell you what to do in them. Do you have an obvious place to pray?

OBSERVATIONS FROM A FRIEND

# Building Her Faith

Your friend is expecting God. When you go to her house, in what ways does she make you feel welcome?

_____
_____
_____
_____

When your friend talks about God, what's the context? Where do you think she usually notices God's love for her?

_____
_____
_____
_____

Often we give to God the same way we would give to friends we love. If your friend were coming over to your house for a visit, what would you ask her to bring? What would you imagine she would bring if you told her to just bring herself? The answers to these questions can give clues as to how she likes to pray. If your friend brings you music, her prayer life might flourish when she sings or listens to music. If your friend brings you food she's grown, she might connect well with God by praying as she works in the garden. If she brings you sweets, she might thrive by connecting with God through giving thanks for the sweetness of life.

If she loves to share books or poems, she might grow in God by offering to Him her love of learning. If she writes you letters, she might also pray most strongly when she writes to God.

Saints are often depicted in art holding a scroll or alongside a speech banner showing a sentence or two of an important part of their testimony to God. If your friend were a saint, what would her scroll say?

If you could give your friend one free hour to do anything she wanted, what do you think she would do? This activity might help you both to see what will build up your friend in faith.

JOURNAL PROMPT

# *God Is with You*

For the next few days, notice your daily routines. What do you do? Where do you go? Do you have a favorite cup or chair? A favorite song? Do you sing or speak in your home? Play? Walk the dog? Do chores? Get ready for bed? Make notes for yourself about what you do and where.

Now, look at your daily routine. God is with you through all of it. How can you act as though you are expecting God to be with you in every room, in every routine, in every conversation and action?

When you have had a day or two to think about these questions, write about your day as though you expect God to be with you in each part of it.

*River ⌢ Piama*

# DRAGON

*Katherine Bolger Hyde*

# *You Are Margaret*

YOU ARE MARGARET. Yesterday you walked in the fresh air and green grass of the countryside, contentedly watching over your foster mother's sheep as you prayed and glorified God. But today, because your beauty has tempted a powerful man, you must pray to God from prison.

You huddle in a corner of a dank and airless dungeon cell, your clothing already torn and dirty from the rough way they dragged you here. The packed earth beneath you is damp and smells of mold—and something worse. The stone wall at your back is cold and hard, forcing you to stay in the present rather than slipping into a doze or a comforting daydream. You can see something wriggling out of the corner of your eye. You try not to think about what it might be.

You made the choice to stay true to your chosen Bridegroom, Christ. And this is the result. You have no regrets; you knew this could happen. It's happened to many others who remained faithful to the Crucified One, through horrible tortures and temptations, all the way to death. Your spirit is ready—but your flesh is still just a little bit weak.

And so you pray. You pray to remain firm no matter what happens. You pray the Lord to send His holy angels to protect you, heal you, carry you home. You pray that His will be done, no matter what that might mean, for you long to be united to the One you have chosen.

Yet still that tiny voice in the back of your head whispers its poison. "You don't have to endure this. You could survive. You could live in the lap of luxury for the rest of your life. Think of it—the gold-embroidered robes, the finest linen sheets, the rarest fruits from the ends of the empire. Armies of servants to fulfill your every whim. Nothing to do but enjoy each day to the fullest. All you have to do is accept Olymbrios as your husband. What's so bad about that? A few months in his bed and he'll get tired of you, move on to another woman and leave you in peace. Your mother married a pagan—a priest, no less. And she was saved. Your Jesus will understand. He'll forgive you. You're only a weak and feeble woman, after all. A child, even. Fifteen years old! That's no age to die. You've got your whole life ahead of you. Just say that little word, 'yes.' Then everything will be fine."

You try to shut your ears to that voice, but you can't, because it's inside you. You pray harder. You sing softly, then louder and louder, every hymn and psalm you can think of, but still you can't drown it out. "Just say yes," it whispers, "and you'll be sleeping on a feather bed in no time."

At last you can take no more. "My Lord!" you cry out from the depths of your anguish. "Let this demon no longer torment me! Let me see it face to face, that I may conquer it by Your power!"

Immediately you're aghast. What have you asked for? To see the devil face to face? Do you really have enough faith to stare into the eyes of the Adversary and not die on the spot?

But the Lord knows your faith, your strength, better than you know yourself. And He answers your call.

In one corner of your cell appears a blackish, writhing thing.

It's dark in the dungeon, you can't see clearly—what is it? Then a lick of flame curls out of its mouth, lighting up the cell like a flash of lightning, and suddenly you know.

It's a dragon.

Not a large dragon; the cell could not hold a full-sized one. But size hardly seems to matter. It's a dragon! It has foul, stinking, roasting-hot breath and glinting metallic scales and horrible leathery wings like a gigantic bat. It opens its mouth to roar, and you see its teeth like great spikes, like the bars of a cage, like the gates of doom ready to close upon you.

Your courage deserts you. "O Lord, what have I done? How can I defeat this thing? You must do it, Lord. Destroy it by Your power. I can do nothing."

You cower back into your corner, but you can go no farther. The dragon looms before you, growing bigger until it fills every inch of the space. Its giant mouth gapes above you, then—oh, horror!—engulfs your head, your torso, your squeezed-up-tight knees.

You are inside the dragon.

You try to breathe, but there is little air, and what you can grasp at is so fetid it makes you retch. Somehow through the panicked fog in your brain you remember the story of Jonah in the belly of the whale. A whale's maw sounds more spacious than a dragon's, but perhaps no less putrid. What did Jonah do? Oh, right, he prayed.

So you pray. "O Lord Jesus Christ, deliver me from this dragon by the power of Your Cross!" And without even thinking what you're doing, you pull the small wooden cross on its leather thong from your neck and thrust it as far as you can reach, until it touches flesh.

And then the world explodes.

Or that's what it feels like. But actually, it was only the dragon that exploded. The cell walls still rise whole around you; your limbs are still in their proper places; you feel no pain. But the remnants of the hellish creature lie at your feet, its ripped belly gaping.

And you are free. You have triumphed. You are victorious by the power of the Cross.

You scramble to your feet and stretch your cramped limbs. But you've barely begun to sing your praise to Christ when you see the other thing.

The dragon was only the opening act, the sidekick. Your real enemy crouches in the opposite corner, grinning horribly. His face is a grotesque parody of a human face, his form more distorted than that of the most pitifully deformed infant. His blackened lips draw back over crazily crooked, wickedly pointed teeth. His breath is even worse than the dragon's.

"So, you've killed my dragon, have you, little girl?" he hisses at you. "I really didn't think you'd manage it. I'm impressed." He licks his lips and leers at you. "In fact, I wouldn't mind having you on my side. All that courage, and beauty too. You'd be quite a catch." He reaches twisted, shriveled arms toward you, and you involuntarily step back. "Come, join me. I can give you even more than that fool Olymbrios could. I can give you the world. Every single king and kingdom, trampled under your pretty little feet just like my poor dragon. Come on. You know you want to." He gives you a laborious wink.

You shudder, not in the least tempted now. You are seeing him for what he really is, this demon who has been whispering so seductively in the far corners of your mind. You might almost have believed he could offer you beauty as long as he was hidden like that; but now, he's out in the open, his hideousness right there in front of you, undisguised. And the light and glory of Christ, your heavenly Bridegroom, shine unhindered in sole possession of your mind.

"By the power of the Lord Jesus Christ, the only-begotten Son of God, and of the eternal Father and the Holy Spirit, I command you—go back from whence you came!" And with your foot, your pretty little foot, you boldly shove the demon's neck to the floor and stamp on it.

And then, in a puff of sulfurous smoke that leaves you gagging, the demon is gone. And so are your doubts, your fears, your hesitation. You stand victorious in the midst of your dungeon, your arms raised to heaven, singing at the top of your voice: "Alleluia! The Lord shall reign forever!"

Tomorrow can bring what it may. You will soon be united with your Bridegroom, and all shall be well.

ON THE LIFE OF THE SAINT

# Margaret

SAINT MARGARET—OR SAINT Marina of Antioch, as she is more commonly known in the Orthodox Church—is one of the many early martyrs about whom little is actually known but much has been invented to make up the deficiency. The story of Margaret and the dragon is a part of her life that is generally considered to be apocryphal but which nevertheless frequently appears in her iconography. Sometimes she is depicted standing over the dragon, spearing it with a long-stemmed cross; sometimes we see her emerging from the dragon's maw, holding her cross aloft. My own opinion is, if we can credit St. George with slaying a demon in the form of a dragon, why not St. Margaret? Their power is not in their own bodily strength but in the might of the Cross. A woman might slay such a dragon as easily as a man.

The accepted facts of Margaret's life are quickly told. She was born in Antioch in Pisidia in the late third century and grew up under the persecutions of Diocletian. Her father was a pagan priest and her mother a Christian. Margaret's mother died while she was quite young, and the baby was given to a nurse to raise. The nurse was also Christian and raised Margaret in the Faith. When her father discovered his daughter was a follower of Christ, he disowned her. Her nurse took her into her home in the country and loved her like a daughter.

While there, the teenaged Margaret helped to tend the sheep. One charming Renaissance painting depicts her standing in a field, surrounded by sheep, spinning with a drop spindle. The composition of the painting makes it look at first glance as if Margaret is spinning her wool directly off the back of the sheep standing next to her. But on closer examination, one can see the drop spindle hanging below the sheep's belly.

Alas, however, this pastoral idyll was not to endure. Margaret, like all Christian virgins of old who vowed to dedicate their lives to Christ, was exceedingly beautiful; and like so many beautiful young women, she was destined to be discovered and sought as a bride by a powerful man—in this case, Olymbrios, the pagan governor of Pisidia. While out riding with his men, he caught sight of Margaret tending her sheep and vowed to have her, either as wife or as concubine.

Margaret of course refused, as she had already given herself to her heavenly Bridegroom. Did Olymbrios say "Thank you kindly for considering my offer, ma'am," tip his hat, and continue politely on his way? He did not. Hearing that she was a Christian, he needed no further excuse to command his men to arrest her and throw her into prison.

At this point, the dragon and the demon come into the story. Perhaps such creatures did appear to Margaret in her darkest hour. It wouldn't have been the first time a saint had seen these inhabitants of the invisible realm take shape to taunt and tempt her at a time when hope seemed thin and rescue impossible. But whether her struggle was with enemies visible or invisible, whether she conquered with a tangible cross or more simply by her faith and reliance on Christ, Margaret's resolve remained firm. The next day she faced her torturers determined to suffer and die for her Bridegroom, if need be, rather than renounce Him for another.

The nature of the tortures to which Margaret was subjected varies between accounts. Some say that on the first day her flesh was torn from her bones, but overnight she was visited by angels, who healed her completely. Her hagiographers are more or less unanimous that after this, she was sent to be burned, but the flames did not touch her.

Margaret called out to her Lord to grant her the grace of baptism before she died. Olymbrios, hearing this, commanded that she be drowned in a cauldron. But a dove came down from heaven bearing a golden crown and placed it on Margaret's head. Her bonds fell away, and, glorifying God, she emerged unscathed from her unconventional baptismal font.

Many of the onlookers (sources say fifteen thousand, but this is probably typical ancient hyperbole) were converted at the sight of Margaret's sufferings. The furious governor, determined to end this debacle once and for all, commanded that Margaret and all her converts be beheaded. At first the executioner refused to carry out his task, having also been brought to share Margaret's faith. But she told him he must perform this duty as the will of God if he wished to be saved. And so St. Margaret went to meet her Lord.

Because of the story of her conquering a demon, Margaret's protection is often invoked in cases of demonic possession. In the West, she came to be associated with childbirth because of its resemblance to her bursting forth from the dragon's belly. She has historically been asked to intercede for mothers—for their safety in childbirth—and for infants, that they be born healthy and free of defects. Some longer medieval versions of Margaret's life record her imploring Christ to protect in childbirth all who would read her life, call upon her name, or even have her written life bound against their bodies during labor.

Saint Margaret was especially revered by St. Frideswide, the founder and patroness of Oxford, England. When attempting to escape from her own unwanted suitor, Frideswide implored St.

Margaret's aid, and the suitor was blinded so he could not find her. After he repented, Frideswide prayed to St. Margaret again, and a holy well appeared. Frideswide bathed her reformed suitor's eyes in the water of the well, and his sight was restored. This well still exists in the yard of St. Margaret's Church in the village of Binsey, near Oxford. I myself had the blessing of visiting the church on St. Margaret's feast day and being sprinkled with the water from her well.

Margaret is said to have reposed in the year 304. Her memory is celebrated on July 17 in the Orthodox Church.

STEPPING FURTHER INTO THE STORY

# *Battling the Ugly Beast*

It's a little odd that I should identify with St. Margaret. On the surface, we don't have much in common. She lived seventeen centuries ago and halfway around the world from my home in California. She was a virgin; I'm a wife, mother, and grandmother. She was the daughter of a pagan priest and a Christian mother who died young; I'm the daughter of an agnostic editor and a Christian mother who raised me largely on her own. Margaret reposed at fifteen as a martyr for Christ; I've survived into my sixties and am more likely to die from illness, accident, or just plain old age.

But there is one thing Margaret and I have in common: fighting dragons. Metaphorical dragons, to be sure, but no less dangerous for all that. Margaret's dragon was the embodiment of a demon, whom she slew by the power of the Cross. My dragon, though invisible, is lamentably familiar to many of my sisters: in our day, it goes by the name of Depression. Its close relations, who sometimes tag along with it, are known by names such as Despondency, Acedia, and Despair.

Depression is a subtle dragon, insidious, persistent. It may lurk inactive for months or years before rearing its frightful head to torment me once more. Sometimes I think I've slain it, only to see it come back with renewed power.

I was about the same age as Margaret when Depression first attacked me. He feeds on hormones, among other things, and teenaged girls are among his favorite delicacies. All through my childbearing years he lurked and slithered and prowled on the borders of my mind and heart, leaping on me when I was at my most vulnerable. And so many things could make me vulnerable: hormonal shifts, poor diet, lack of sleep or exercise. The isolation I often felt in those middle years, when I was living in a foreign-feeling place and struggling through an abusive marriage that would ultimately fail. Grief over my mother's death, divorce, single motherhood—all were sweetest honey to Depression's depraved and ravenous tongue.

When I remarried and moved back to the West Coast where I felt more at home, Depression retreated for a while. I was loved, I was accepted in my community, I was busy, I was useful. But then I had another baby, and a few years later another, and that wily old dragon saw his opportunity again. The postpartum months are his truffles and caviar. Life continued to happen, with financial crises, health crises, my father moving in with us and later dying, the inevitable tensions arising in my marriage, and ultimately the once-again-crazy hormones of menopause. Depression lapped it all up and begged for more.

Finally, the burdens of life eased off. Menopause was finished; the budget was balanced; the kids were through school (no more carpools! Hooray!). I began publishing novels, my lifelong dream. Depression went off to sulk in a corner for a little while.

But not for long. My nest emptied temporarily; my dearest friend got very sick; my love affair with writing threatened to grow cold. I began to wonder what was the point of me. And wouldn't you know it, that old dragon pricked up its ears and licked its lips, ready for another meal. Unlike us (in our mortal bodies, at least), dragons live forever. They don't get tired or weaken, no matter how long we make them wait. They are always lurking, ready to pounce one more time, hoping this time they will be able to devour us completely.

purportedly swallowed by her dragon, and it is as if Depression has swallowed me; but in fact it lives inside me, which makes it even more difficult to conquer. I've tried all the weapons: therapy, drugs, natural supplements, lifestyle changes, fulfilling hobbies, positive thinking, thanksgiving, prayer. Each one makes a dent in the armor, scrapes a scale or two off the dragon's side, douses its flames for a little while, but none has ever been able to quench it permanently.

I think that's because Depression has sunk its steely claws into every aspect of my being—body, mind, heart, soul, spirit. Each weapon I wield briefly pries loose one claw but leaves the others untouched. When I turn my attention to a second claw, the first sinks in again. And the most insidious thing about this dragon is that he saps my mental and physical energy, my very power to battle him. The more I need to fight him, the less I'm able to. Prayer, in any form other than a spontaneous cry for help, feels unattainable. When the dragon really has me in his clutches, I can barely get out of bed.

Margaret was victorious over her dragon, which I imagine may have been called Wavering or Doubt, by virtue of her great faith in the power of the Cross. Thus I must believe that victory is possible for me as well. If I have faith, the power of Christ is sufficient to pry out all of Depression's claws at once and banish the dragon forever from my life.

But I must also accept that this instant and total victory, this banishment, may not be God's will for me. Saint Paul had his thorn in the flesh, which God would not remove because it served for Paul's humility and ultimate salvation. Perhaps Depression is my thorn. Perhaps what is required of me is simply to keep fighting, keep prying loose those claws, dousing those flames, scraping off those scales. If I can keep fighting in God's strength, perhaps

Depression will ultimately grow tired of the buffeting and slink off to lick his wounds.

Most recently, the pandemic, with its attendant isolation and disruption of my church life, has given Depression some of his tastiest morsels yet. But for the moment, as I write this, he's sated, sleeping it off. I have a child back in the nest for a while, I'm busy, I'm useful, my writing mojo has returned. If I can use this respite to develop good habits—nutritious eating, regular exercise, sunshine, good sleep, keeping busy, keeping up with friends, praying and giving thanks on a daily basis, lots of reading, writing, and knitting, not so much screen time—perhaps I'll find myself well armed when he wakes again.

It will take some time, much dedication and perseverance. But eventually, I hope and pray, my dragon's fires will burn out, and he will be humiliated. You will see me looking like Margaret in some of her icons, standing victorious over the dragon that has tormented me all my life, plunging the sword of the Cross into his belly with a serene smile on my angelically beaming face. The victory, of course, will be not mine, but Christ's.

You may be fortunate enough not to be acquainted with the dragon called Depression. But I think most of us have some dragon of our own. Perhaps yours is Doubt, or Fear, or Pride, or Anger. It could be called Gluttony or Greed or Envy or Discouragement. Or your dragon might be Anxiety, or Trauma, or one of the numerous brothers Phobia. I myself have a subsidiary dragon, a sidekick of the main one, called Sloth. (He's still plaguing me because he's too lazy to leave.)

Whatever your dragon or dragons might be, try praying to St. Margaret to help you conquer them in the power of Christ. Persevere in faith, and maybe someday, the canon of saints will include Saint You, the Dragonslayer.

PERSONAL SURVEY

## Here There Be Dragons

Do you identify with St. Margaret's struggle? What dragon(s) do you fight on a daily basis?

_____
_____
_____

How would you describe your degree of victory over these dragons? Can you think of any additional weapons you might try?

_____
_____
_____

Whom do you know who will stand with you in fighting your dragons? Saint Margaret fought with no help but that of Christ and His Cross (the most important help, to be sure!), but most of us have other resources as well—our spouse, friends, perhaps professionals of various kinds, a spiritual father, the community of the Church. How can you call these comrades-in-arms to your aid?

_____
_____
_____
_____

Though most of us will probably not face physical martyrdom, we all endure the minor martyrdom of life in the world, whether as wives, mothers, or single women, working in the world or at home. How can you stand firm in your commitment to Christ as you face the martyrdom of the everyday?

Many stories of virgin martyrs include their being tempted to betray Christ for an earthly bridegroom who offers them wealth and power. Taking this symbolically, what sometimes tempts you to betray your faith? How do you resist?

## OBSERVATIONS FROM A FRIEND

# *Lending a Trusty Sword*

Can you identify any dragons your friend is fighting right now? How can you help her in her struggle? Brainstorm together about weapons she might use.

_____
_____
_____
_____

What ways do you see in which your friend has been victorious? Encourage her by pointing these out to her.

_____
_____
_____

Does your struggle with your own dragons make it harder or easier to help your friend? Struggle can make us more compassionate, but it can also wear us out. As you and your friend struggle together, each of you will have times when you need more help and times when you are more available to help the other. Talk about this together.

_____
_____
_____

The final victory may not come this side of heaven, but we each achieve little victories along the way. How can you help your friend celebrate these victories?

Do you ever witness your friend being tempted to abandon her everyday martyrdom? How can you help her to stand firm?

JOURNAL PROMPT

# *Recognizing Dragons*

*Thou shalt tread upon the lion and adder:
the young lion and the dragon shalt thou trample under feet.*
—Psalm 91:13, KJV

THROUGHOUT SCRIPTURE, AT least in the older translations, dragons are identified with evil. Sometimes, as in the verses above, the dragons may be taken literally as dangerous creatures that God will enable us to conquer by His power (though of course we may also take them metaphorically). At other times, as in Revelation 12, the dragon is directly identified with Satan.

Up until modern times, dragons continued to be portrayed as powerful, evil creatures that could only be slain by great courage, strength, and purity of heart. But in our relativistic age, in many fantasy stories and rewritten fairy tales, the firm distinction between good and evil, black and white, has been abandoned as "unrealistic." Traditionally evil beings of all sorts have been revisited, humanized, portrayed sometimes as complex and misunderstood, sometimes as wise although dangerous, and sometimes even as cute, friendly, and fundamentally good.

But something important is lost when we paint pure evil in shades of gray or bleach it entirely. If we don't recognize evil for what it is, how can we fight it? Is this literary trend not just one more way in which Satan disguises himself as an angel of light?

Reflect on the disguises under which evil appears in your own life and the lives of your family. Have you been deceived into thinking certain dragons are tame and manageable, perhaps sleeping? Ask God to give you discernment of evil as well as the strength, courage, and faith to fight against it.

# FLOWER

*Melissa Elizabeth Naasko*

# *You Are Casilda de Toledo*

This is your chance, Casilda. You might never have another. You take a deep breath and feel it catch in your throat; sometimes it aches to breathe and swallow. It has been so long since your brother, Almoain, died in these hideous battles with the Christians here in Toledo. The silence he left behind is almost unbearable. You just want to feel the warmth of his hand under yours or hear his ringing laugh, but there is nothing now. He sleeps forever, and he took his warmth and his voice with him.

Your father will never be the same. When Almoain died, your father was incensed like never before, and there may never be peace again. Emir Aldermon is not a man to be trifled with; he is a man of action. This makes what you intend to do tonight incredibly reckless. This is why your heart pounds in your chest so loudly that you can hear it. You are terrified to go but more terrified to stay here in your rooms, because you need answers. The difficulty is that you do not yet know what the questions are. You are compelled to go, pulled by forces that you cannot understand.

Years ago, your tutors exposed you to the cultural riches of the world through the gift of reading. You learned about these Christians through the stories of their holy men and women. One story told of a woman who followed her father into a solitary life devoted to prayer to the Christian God. This daughter was not afraid of her father, who seemed to be a man of mercy. Perhaps there is more to these Christians than your father knows. Then again, perhaps you are foolish. Your brother is dead, after all, dead because of these Christians. You should not forget that or pretend as if you could. You should not do this thing. You should not go to the prison.

Still, you plot. Your father has left the palace, and you prepare to make your way to the only place you are forbidden to see. You are too afraid to let this opportunity pass.

You have said nothing about this to your sister, Zoraida. Perhaps she would follow you into this folly, but more than likely she would be less foolish than you are. If caught, the price you must pay will be extraordinary. You cannot risk telling her—this is something you will have to keep back. In a way, you have also lost your own voice. There is so much silence in these long centuries of war.

Your father knows of your fascination with the prisoners; he is no fool. Why do you want to see them? Why do you want to speak to them? What can they tell you? Would you even want to know what they have to say? Your brother is dead, and those prisoners cannot bring him back. They cannot give you back his voice. They cannot let you run your fingers through his dark hair just one last time. All good things are lost, and all that remains is fear. Still, you pack up the bread and wrap it in the folds of your heavy silk skirts. You feel unable to stop yourself. You must hear what they have to say.

You make your way to the prison. You know where it is, but you have never gone that way; it is forbidden. You have never dared to cross your father until this moment. Each step brings you closer to the prison, closer to whatever answers lie there, and closer to shattering your own obedience. Your hands shake, and they rustle the fabric you hold. You take in a halting breath and try to steady your hands so you do not drop the bread you carry.

You stumble. You are weak. A hemorrhage has plagued you for years. This is what took your mother from you. Almoain's voice is not the only one you miss. You hope that you will be healed, but more likely you will die. If so, then disobeying your father tonight won't mean anything. Whatever consequences you face, they will be temporary. You will escape them through your own death.

Finally, you reach the prison gate. You stand there quietly, hoping that you look confident if not defiant, but you are exhausted and consumed with doubt. You cannot bring yourself to speak first, so you wait to be addressed. You tremble, and not from the chill.

"What have you, Casilda? There, in your skirts."

You had not considered what you would say about this. You thought only of finding the courage to come to the prison. Now you are here, and you do not know what to do. You have no words. You stand perfectly still, dumbfounded.

"What have you, Casilda?"

Your mind races, but you cannot seem to find any answers there. The soldier takes a step toward you, and you utter the only word that comes to mind.

"Roses."

The soldier is confused. He steps toward you and asks, "You have roses?"

He reaches for your hands. You are visibly shaking now. This was a stupid thing to do. There is nothing to be learned here that is worth the price of being caught bringing bread to the prisoners. You are so angry with yourself that your eyes begin to fill with hot tears. The soldier reaches for your hands, and he pulls them apart to see what you carry.

"Roses," you say again in stunned surprise. You stop shaking. Your skirts are indeed filled with flowers and not the bread you placed in them. You look up at that guard, who shakes his head as he opens the gate. You pass through and pause when you hear the door lock behind you.

The Christians cannot eat roses, and you have nothing to give them now. In the dim light you open your hands once more and see bread. You move closer to the light and look again. Bread. Your skirts are filled with bread. Those hot tears come back, but for an entirely different reason this time.

You lift your head and allow your eyes to adjust to the darkness of the prison. For all that you have planned, you have not prepared for this moment. All you have is a skirt full of bread and a heart full of pain. Somehow you know, deep in that broken heart, that the answers you need are here in this prison. You will have to look until you find them. There is only one thing you do know, and that is that nothing will ever be the same again.

You breathe deeply once more, then step into the darkness.

ON THE LIFE OF THE SAINT

# Casilda

WE KNOW PRECIOUS little about St. Casilda. We know that she was the daughter of a Muslim emir or king in Moorish Spain. She was born in the eleventh century prior to the Great Schism and lived during the extended period of time when the Moors ruled substantial parts of Spain, including the area surrounding Toledo. We know little of her life or of her family, but the *Acta Sanctorum*, a vast and extensive encyclopedia of the lives of saints compiled over centuries, fortunately provides some details of her life. She is also included in the *Martyrologium Hispanum* assembled by historian Juan Tamayo de Salazar in the seventeenth century. This collection specifically focused on Christian history in Spain.

Her father's name appears differently in different texts, and he might have been called Aldermon, Al-Mumun, or Almacrin. Given that we are looking at Spanish corruptions of Arabic names from an era without a codified system of spelling, this is unsurprising. She had a brother, Almoain, who died in the Reconquista, the wars between the Muslims and Christians which lasted from 780 until 1491, when the Christian kingdoms were unified. Her sister was born Zoraida but was baptized Yzabel (Elizabeth) when she converted to Christianity.

Casilda was well educated as a young woman and apparently in her studies came across the stories of St. Marina the Monk, a woman who disguised herself then lived as a monk in what is now Lebanon. It's recorded that Casilda found St. Marina's story especially evocative; perhaps it made her sympathetic toward her father's Christian prisoners.

Casilda was forbidden to visit the prison but would sneak off to do just that when her father left the palace. Moved by compassion, she would take food, water, and medicines to the Christians. The stories vary as to whether she was confronted by her father or a soldier guarding the cells, but apparently her movements were not above suspicion. While carrying bread in the folds of her upheld skirts, she was stopped and asked what she carried. She answered that she carried roses. When she was compelled to hold open her skirt, it appeared that she really did carry only roses, so she was permitted to pass. Some accounts state that this happened repeatedly—on her visits her parcels were always inspected, and only roses were found. Some other accounts state that she did not work alone but brought along a lady's maid who carried meat in her skirts. Casilda remained Muslim for some time, but her conversion to Christianity began with these visits.

Her mother had apparently succumbed to hemorrhagic bleeding, and Casilda suffered from the same condition. She could not be healed by the Muslim court physicians, because of either their lack of skill or her unwillingness to be treated, so her life was in grave danger. She had heard from the prisoners that healing waters were to be found in the Christian kingdom of La Bureba, specifically Briviesca, in northern Spain. She pleaded with her father to allow her to make the pilgrimage in order to drink this holy water and be cured. He finally conceded and contacted the Christian king of Castile to request a safe passage for his daughter.

Once she had permission, Casilda made the journey to the shrine of San Vicente de Briviesca in Castile. There she drank the water of the lake. Some stories say that her horse reared up as she passed by, and she fell into the water. Other accounts suggest that she approached the lake on her knees and drank voluntarily. Either way, having drunk the water, she was not only fully healed but had a fervent desire to be baptized and stay at the shrine. She never returned home to her family.

Casilda became an anchoress at the shrine and chose to live a solitary life in the surrounding hills. She lived ascetically in a cave and devoted her life to prayer and penance. The people of the nearby village came to love her very much and wanted to help make her more comfortable. They decided to build her a modest home at the base of the hill to comfort her and keep her close to others. But every night, while the villagers slept, all the work that they completed on her house was moved to the top of the hill near the cave. After their materials were relocated repeatedly, they gave up. Believing that angels were interrupting their work, the villagers decided it was the will of God that Santa Casilda live at the top of the hill, and they built the house there. She lived to a very advanced age; some say she was one hundred years old when she reposed in about 1050, again prior to the Great Schism. Afterward, her body was interred in her home, which was expanded into a small shrine for her relics.

Santa Casilda was known for her compassion for Christians while a Muslim and her compassion for Muslims as a Christian. Her intercession is invoked for the healing of menstrual dysfunctions and infertility. Despite being relatively unknown in Orthodoxy, she is beloved in Spain, particularly northern Spain. She is not venerated on the Roman calendar but is commemorated on April 9 in the Orthodox Church.

Saint Casilda of Toledo, pray for us!

STEPPING FURTHER INTO THE STORY

# A Dinner Party

MY SPIRITUAL FATHER once told me that coming to know the saints is like meeting people at a dinner party. When I think about it, this is exactly what it's like.

We have heard about some of the saints, and we make an effort to introduce ourselves to them. We want to get to know them, so we find them. We talk to them. We tell them about ourselves. We might even look them up on the Internet before the party so that we might know them better. We always knew we would be good friends, and we are.

Other saints are the friends of friends, the ones we hear about for days, weeks, months, and sometimes even years before we make an effort to get to know them. At the party, our friends introduce us to them and help with the conversation until we find enough commonality that we can carry on alone. These saints are the friends we didn't know we needed, and we are grateful for the introduction.

Some saints find us. They know who we are, and they seek us out. We might immediately bond with them and become fast friends. Sometimes, they have to persist because we are too busy on our phones, but at some point, we look up and actually connect with them. We find that they have been waiting for us, for perhaps a very long time. These are the easiest saints to overlook. We have to be won over by their quiet patience. But as enduring as their fortitude is, the strength of their love is even greater.

Making friends among the great multitude of saints who sit close to God is a gift. It is time well spent, and in the end, it doesn't matter how we met. All that matters is that friendship. I am grateful to call St. Casilda my friend and grateful for the opportunity to get to know her, to grow closer to her. I am immediately drawn into her story for so many reasons. I can't decide if she was a friend of a friend, since we were introduced on the basis of my Spanish background, or if she found me. Either way, now that we are friends, I will tell others about her.

That is what I am doing now. I am gathering my friends together at a dinner party to tell you about this amazing woman, St. Casilda, and her strength and her courage and her compassion. I know that she will love you, and I know that you will love her and learn from her, especially during difficult times. We all have moments in our lives when we can feel the current shifting, knowing that we are seconds from being carried away by the flood and that our lives will never be the same again. Who better to hold our hands in these moments, when we are too scared to move forward but also too afraid to step back? Casilda knows how hard it is to move closer to God when we are afraid, and she wants to be there for us.

So many of you dear friends are suffering from infertility or menstrual disorders, and you want healing and hope. Saint Casilda understands. Her mother died from hemorrhage, and she struggled with it for a significant part of her own life. She knows how you suffer, and she wants to be present for you, to listen to you cry and complain, and to pray with you. She wants to go to God and plead for you. Who doesn't need a friend like that?

Some of you have deep fractures in your family lives, or you suffer following the deaths of loved ones whom you miss so much that you are exhausted. Working through grief takes a herculean amount of effort, and sometimes you don't have the strength to keep putting one foot in front of another. Casilda wants to be that shoulder to lean on when your own strength is spent. You need her, and I have to make sure that you get to know her. You need someone to take your hand when you feel like you are drowning and are too tired to swim any longer.

Saint Casilda is real. I want you to know that, and not just know it, but sense it deep in your soul. The saints are very much like us, but ourselves shaped by our better angels. We need their love and their guidance and their extraordinary patience as they hold our hands and walk with us amid the slings and arrows of this broken world. They have braved this path before us, and they know all the pitfalls. If we follow after them carefully, holding tightly to them, we can navigate this path and find wholeness and healing. Saint Casilda is one such guide. I want you to know her.

I will stay with you. I will help the conversation along, pointing out what you have in common. I will be here, reminding you about the things that you share. I will encourage Casilda to share with you and even prompt you to share your thoughts with her. I know that in the end, you will find a kindred spirit, a friend you didn't know you needed. Eventually, you won't need me here, and I can step back and leave you two to talk and share. I can step away, knowing that you will be gently cared for, in good times and especially in the bad. You have found a lifelong friend, and it makes me so happy.

I always knew you would get on well together.

PERSONAL SURVEY

## *Befores and Afters*

Casilda showed great bravery in facing the guard at the prison. What moments are you facing in which her example of courage can encourage you?

_____
_____
_____
_____

There are moments when we face the reality of our lives changing completely—moments that separate what was before and what came after. What event or events in your life mark your experiences in this way, separating your "befores" and "afters"?

_____
_____
_____
_____

Casilda knew the prisoners had answers she needed to begin her lifelong journey to Christianity. Who in your life has been instrumental in helping you become who you are today?

_____
_____
_____
_____

Like those Christian prisoners, we are ordinary people who find ourselves in ordinary moments that actually turn out to be extraordinary. How have you touched the lives of others in an unexpected way?

Can you think of an instance in your life when God was repeatedly trying to get your attention and draw your activity somewhere other than where you had planned to be?

We all have some kind of physical or spiritual illness that plagues us, dogs our steps. What healing can you ask St. Casilda to pray for along with you?

Like any other woman's, Casilda's life was complicated and full of many different kinds of events. When you think about her life, what single moment stands out to you?

OBSERVATIONS FROM A FRIEND

# Speaking to Our Sisters

Our friends are our sisters in Christ. We can flesh out an understanding of these relationships by thinking about the relationship between Casilda and her sister. Casilda was able to lead her sister into her Christian Faith in a time and place where this could have resulted in a punishment of death. When you think about your friend, how has one of you led the other to a place where you both needed to be? How did the example of one give strength to the other?

---
---
---
---

Sometimes our losses unite us to other women. Casilda and Yzabel lost both their mother and brother, and in converting risked losing not only their relationship with their father but even their own lives. When you think about your relationship with your friend, are there losses you have shared that brought you closer together?

---
---
---
---

We don't know how or when Casilda first spoke about Christianity with Yzabel, but we do know that it happened. Are there things you have been waiting to share with your friend?

Casilda experienced an incredible transformation from a wealthy and privileged Muslim princess to a pious Christian. This was for the greater glory of God and for her own salvation, but it was certainly a painful process. What experiences are you or your friend undergoing that will ultimately be transformative, even if painful?

JOURNAL PROMPT

# Seeking Hidden Treasure

*"But seek first the kingdom of God and His righteousness, and all these things shall be added to you."* (Matthew 6:33)

CASILDA'S JOURNEY INTO Christianity and then into sainthood began with seeking healing—physical healing for her constant hemorrhage and spiritual healing for a life she sensed was not what God wanted for her. In the Bible and throughout Christian history, physical illnesses are an expression or symbol of spiritual ones. Physical illnesses are real, but at their true source lie the consequences of the problem of evil. Casilda's healing on both levels came through water—first the miraculous waters at the Shrine of San Vicente de Briviesca, which healed her body, and then the waters of baptism, which healed her soul.

Where in your own life have you seen this story play out? What is an instance where you have become aware of illness or dis-ease of some sort (emotional, physical, or spiritual), and then experienced healing, particularly through water? It doesn't have to be a grand experience like escaping your father's kingdom. It can be something ordinary, like having a sore back and receiving comfort in a hot bath or wanting to escape the heat of summer by slipping into a swimming pool. Think about the ways in which God heals our small wounds by providing small comforts. Our lives have many moments in which we are able to share in the unfolding of God's mercy, but we are seldom aware of them.

*Flower* ❦ *Casilda*

# HOME

*Melinda Johnson*

# *You Are You*

You will heave stones over the precipice and build a cathedral, but you are not Morwenna.

You will closet yourself against the onslaught and chant your hymn, but you are not Kassiani.

You will trust yourself to the impossible and preach the word of God, but you are not Ia.

You will listen to your dream and cast down idols, but you are not Nino.

You will set between your household and the world the power and love of God, but you are not Piama.

You will triumph in prison over hideous dragons, but you are not Margaret.

You will bring unexpected salvation upon yourself by feeding the hungry, but you are not Casilda.

You are you.

CHRISTIAN SALVATION IS A PARADOX. You are created in the image of God, and you are the only one of your incarnation who will ever exist. Yet each human being in the whole past and future course of our eternity can truly say the same. You work out your own salvation in fear and trembling, but you receive it in the community of every faithful worker. You are one and many, individual and multitude. So are we all.

The seven holy women you have encountered in this journey are your sisters in Christ, as you are theirs. Their voices pray with the triumphant choir, the cloud of witnesses whose feet trod the path we are still seeking. With prayer, study, and a creative spirit, we invited ourselves to consider these seven women from their own perspective, although we know that as we are individuals, so are Morwenna, Kassiani, and Ia, Nino, Piama, Margaret, and Casilda. Except in sympathy, God grants us only our own eyes on the world.

Storytelling, imagination, artistry, all the tools and fruits of our creativity can strengthen or weaken our spiritual life. Saint Barsanuphius tells us, "Poets and artists who are satisfied only by the delights experienced through art are like people who arrive at the doors of the Royal Palace but do not go in to the bridal feast, although they are invited to do so." Ponder this. Writing and reading from a saint's perspective is fascinating, refreshing, and mystical, but literary enjoyment, even with the spice of sanctity, still abandons us outside the doors of Paradise. If we are satisfied only with these delights, we are lost. We will not step through those doors in any shoes but our own.

Yet the solemn warning comes on the wings of an invitation. It is not the poetry or art that is to blame. It is the choice to relish only the surface of great beauty, to linger in the senses despite the powerful urging to transcend them in search of that greater beauty. Read the saint's words again. "Poets and artists . . . are invited to . . . go in to the bridal feast." There is victory to be wrested from temptation. When poetry and art carry us near the doors of the Royal Palace, let us stand up and enter into the joy of our Lord.

The words you wrote in this book are far more important than those we wrote. Your words are your work. Sometimes they are the memory of effort and a chance to reflect upon it. Sometimes, the words themselves are the effort, the epiphany granted to a spirit yearning to grow. Blunt or beautiful, your words are not the glittering shallows.

This book began with four short stories—You Are Morwenna, You Are Kassiani, You Are Ia, You Are Nino. The more the book grew in my mind, the more exhausted I felt thinking about writing it. One day, I realized I could ask my friends to help. Like life, writing is something you think you will do alone. You think you will learn about writing from other people and then do the writing by yourself. This is true and not true. Writing, like salvation, happens alone and in community. As I collected friends and gave them saints to write about, we began to say we were following the "Holy Spirit theory of writing," by which we meant that we would let the book be whatever it wished to be. We would follow wherever we were led.

Some paths are only visible when you look back along the way you have come. Gazing over our shoulders, we discovered that the book's creation exemplifies its message. It is a unity and a multitude, a collection of individuals whose choiring voices share one clear melody. The parts would never have come into existence without the whole, and the whole has no existence aside from the loving creation of each part.

We offer you these stories of Morwenna, Kassiani, Ia, Nino, Piama, Margaret, and Casilda not to replace our own identities or yours, but to draw our friendship with these seven holy women out of the ink and paper, out of the separate world of intellectual facts, into the living space of our hearts and memories. In joy and sorrow, we call on those we know for comfort and celebration.

Our friends sustain us. May the holy saints be so known that they too will answer when we call.

# The Women Who Wrote This Book

## *Melinda Johnson*

MELINDA EARNED AN MA IN English literature from the College of William and Mary and a BA in English with minors in journalism and education from the University of Richmond. She is the author of *Letters to Saint Lydia* (Conciliar Press, 2010), *The Other Side of the Bonfire* (Lingua Sacra, 2012), *Shepherding Sam* (Ancient Faith Publishing, 2016), *The Barn and the Book* (AFP, 2018), *Piggy in Heaven* (Paraclete Press, 2019), and *Painting Angels* (AFP, 2020), along with numerous essays. She has led parish, regional, and national retreats for women, teen girls, and Orthodox writers and podcasters, and as the marketing director at Ancient Faith Ministries, she works with Orthodox creatives and researches Orthodox market trends and voices daily. Melinda is a wife, mother, daughter, sister, and friend, and she belongs to a corgi named Ferdinand.

*Saint Lydia is my patron because I heard her name in a Bible reading not long before my baptism and knew she was the one.*

## *Laura S. Jansson*

LAURA IS A PUDDLE-STOMPING, TEA-BREWING, pen-chewing, dough-punching Orthodox Christian. For the past decade and a half, Laura has been supporting growing families as a doula and childbirth educator and has attended scores of births. Her book, *Fertile Ground: A Pilgrimage Through Pregnancy* (AFP, 2019), is a spiritual guidebook for the journey to motherhood for women who want to spend their pregnancy growing in faith as well as in girth. Laura was born in California and has lived in Fiji, Germany, and Serbia. She holds an MA in theology and philosophy from Oxford University and currently resides in the UK with her husband, four children, and an elderly mutt who thinks he is still a puppy.

*My patron saint is Saint Elizabeth, the Mother of the Forerunner. I chose her as a patron when I became Orthodox because my middle name is Elisabeth (with an s). Both she and I can look at a pregnant belly and glimpse the Lord.*

## *Georgia Briggs*

GEORGIA BRIGGS GREW UP NEAR Birmingham, Alabama, listening to her father tell stories stolen from Shakespeare, Bronte, and Orwell. After college, having failed to find Deeper Magic in a wardrobe, she stumbled upon it in the Orthodox Church. In 2016 she released the novel *Icon*, her first publication with Ancient Faith. Now Georgia divides her energies between her family, iconography, and writing. She enjoys singing in the choir at Saint Symeon Orthodox Church in Birmingham.

*I chose St. George for my patron saint because of the important role he played in my conversion and subsequent healing. From my childhood I had loved reading the tale of St. George and the dragon. When I became a catechumen, I learned that St. George was real, that I could in a small way become him by taking his name, and I finally understood that I had to stop surrendering to the dragon and start fighting. I became Georgia in baptism, and through the prayers of St. George I am finally free.*

About the Authors

## Molly Sabourin

MOLLY IS A NATURAL-LIGHT PORTRAIT photographer living in northwest Indiana, where she pours most of her energies into seizing each new day, being a supportive wife and mom, challenging herself artistically, and loving the person in front of her. When she's not behind her camera, Molly is a project manager for Holistic Christian Life and a freelance writer. Her work has been featured as both a podcast and blog on Ancient Faith Radio, and her book, *Close to Home: One Orthodox Mother's Quest for Patience, Peace, and Perseverance*, was published by Ancient Faith in 2008.

*My saint is the Prophetess Anna. We chose her because she shares a feast day with my husband's patron saint, St. Simeon. I love that she was married, and then when she was widowed devoted the latter years of her life to anticipating with great hope the coming of Christ and sharing that hope with others.*

## Anna Neill

ANNA NEILL IS A HISTORIAN, librarian, and artisan who works out her salvation within the mission parish of St. Raphael of Brooklyn (Antiochian) in Fuquay Varina, North Carolina. She earned her BA in history from Hollins University and her master's degree in library and information studies from Wayne State University. She writes for The Brown Dress Project, a blog exploring Orthodox women saints throughout the ages of the Church. Anna and her husband dress in handsewn costumes and participate in early American living-history events along the East Coast. Her favorite role is as godmama to a family of little boys who eagerly anticipate the new bag of library books she brings each week to Liturgy.

*My patron saint is Anna, the mother of the Virgin Mary and grandmother of Christ. My full given name is Annamarie, so why change up a good idea in progress?*

## *Summer Kinard*

SUMMER KINARD IS A GREEK Orthodox Christian, mother of five autistic children, tea lover, classically trained soprano, and author of short stories, four novels, and curricula for active learners. Summer received her master of divinity (summa cum laude, 2003) and master of theology (2005) degrees from Duke University Divinity School. She writes about the practicalities of autistic and spiritual life on her websites and offers free downloads of prayer aids for Christians with communication challenges. Her book *Of Such Is the Kingdom: A Practical Theology of Disability* (AFP, 2019) draws together her study and experience to show how welcoming families with disabilities into the fullness of church life is vital to our salvation. Summer is grateful to be a witness to the transforming grace of God.

*My patron saint is Archangel Michael because "Who is like God?" Also, Michelle has been my given saint name (middle name) since birth.*

## *Katherine Bolger Hyde*

KATHERINE BOLGER HYDE SERVES AS editorial director for Ancient Faith Publishing. Katherine is the author of the Crime with the Classics traditional mystery series for adults, as well as the young-adult fantasy *The Dome-Singer of Falenda* (Waystone Press, 2019) and the picture books *Everything Tells Us about God* (AFP, 2018) and *Lucia, Saint of Light* (AFP, 2009). Her third picture book, tentatively titled *A Taste of Paradise: Stories of Saints and Animals*, is due from AFP in 2021. Her own resident animals, two cats, tolerate the existence of far-from-sanctified Katherine and her husband in the redwood country of California. Katherine has four grown children and four grandchildren.

*My patron is St. Katherine of Alexandria. My parents had the unwitting good sense to name me for a saint with both beauty and brains. Why look any further?*

## *Melissa Elizabeth Naasko*

MELISSA ELIZABETH NAASKO IS THE wife of a priest attached to a ROCOR monastery. They have eleven children and a hobby farm and raise their own meat and dairy. Melissa writes and speaks on Orthodox fasting and parenting and is the author of *Fasting as a Family* (AFP, 2016). She is currently writing a personal memoir, *Coming to Idyll Hands Farm*, for Waystone Press.

*My patron is St. Elizabeth the New Martyr because her relics were in the altar where I was received.*

Ancient Faith Publishing hopes you have enjoyed and benefited from this book. The proceeds from the sales of our books only partially cover the costs of operating our nonprofit ministry—which includes both the work of **Ancient Faith Publishing** and the work of **Ancient Faith Radio**. Your financial support makes it possible to continue this ministry both in print and online. Donations are tax deductible and can be made at www.ancientfaith.com.

To view our other publications,
please visit our website: **store.ancientfaith.com**

Bringing you Orthodox Christian music, readings, prayers, teaching, and podcasts 24 hours a day since 2004 at www.ancientfaith.com